MY LAZARUS LIFE

Based on the Life, Death, and Life of Teresa-Rose Earp

A True Story

Richard Parnes

As Told by Teresa-Rose Earp

ISBN 979-8-89309-899-0 (Paperback)
ISBN 979-8-89309-901-0 (Hardcover)
ISBN 979-8-89309-900-3 (Digital)

Copyright © 2024 Richard Parnes
All rights reserved
First Edition

All rights reserved. No part of this publication may be reproduced, distributed, or transmitted in any form or by any means, including photocopying, recording, or other electronic or mechanical methods without the prior written permission of the publisher. For permission requests, solicit the publisher via the address below.

Covenant Books
11661 Hwy 707
Murrells Inlet, SC 29576
www.covenantbooks.com

Books by Richard Parnes

Fiction
> *The Death Maze*
> *The Death Maze 2: The Other Side*

Spiritual Poetry
> *Peace in Kind*
> *Believe in the Cross*

AUTHOR'S NOTE

I had met Gregory Bain at bible study on a Saturday morning. There were fifteen—maybe eighteen—other individuals who were there to study the Sunday readings and the gospel. Following bible study, we talked for some time as he had heard I was an author and wanted to know what I had written.

After reading my first book, a sci-fi/suspense fiction, he wanted to know more, and we became good friends. He was impressed with the characterizations, the details, and the imagination of the book. He has since bought the sequel and my two spiritual books of poetry.

He came to me a few weeks later and said that I had to stop everything I was doing and meet this friend of his. "She is amazing!" was all he would say before continuing with a bit of her history. "You need to write her biography as I told her about your writings and gave her the first sci-fi-suspense book." Greg had said that he and Teresa-Rose were convinced I was the right person to tackle this true story.

This was something I never thought I could do. I wrote fiction. It was a humbling task to write a biography as I hoped I met all of Teresa-Rose's expectations.

All I wanted to do was get this right. I heard God and Jesus Christ guiding me the entire time I needed to complete this book, as I was a devout believer and attended Mass almost every day.

The title came to me as I was sleeping and listening to the very small voice in my head. After listening to Teresa-Rose for the many hours I interviewed her, I was hopeful everyone who would read this book would be amazed at her story and the veracity of the speech as it was told to me. The best gift I received for writing her biography was the friendship that developed. I would give this book to all who want to know God, the Lord Jesus Christ, and the Holy Ghost. Hopefully, those who are not believers will become interested in learning what it means to be a "believer."

I chose the title "My Lazarus Life" for a reason. The story of Jesus calling for Lazarus to come out from his burial tomb, "which was a cave with a stone laid across the entrance" (John 11:38 NIV), was truly a miraculous testament to Jesus Christ's powers as the Son of God Almighty. Jesus tells Martha, the sister of Lazarus:

> Did I not tell you that if you believe, you will see the glory of God? So they took away the stone. Then Jesus looked up and said "Father, I thank you that you have heard me. I knew that you always hear me, but I said this for the benefit of the people standing here, that they may believe that you sent me." When he had said this, Jesus called out in a loud voice, Lazarus, come out! The dead man came out, his hands and feet wrapped with strips of linen, and a cloth around his face. (John 11:40–44 NIV)

The name Lazarus means "God has helped." In the same manner, God has helped Teresa-Rose Earp.

PROLOGUE

Teresa-Rose Earp was a wonderful person and a beautiful soul. As an OR nurse anesthetist at San Bernardino Hospital Medical Center in San Bernardino, California, she worked tirelessly helping many patients prepare for their surgeries, entering the operating room with them, being wheeled into the operating room, and in post-surgery. Her patients came first. This was her purpose in becoming a nurse.

In 1984, Teresa-Rose became a patient in the operating room, but in Phoenix, Arizona. She had undergone a left upper lobe lobectomy due to San Joaquin Valley fever, wherein spores (a fungus) entered her lungs. She also had a partial fifth-rib resection as the fungus had entered the bone. Despite coughing up blood and bleeding heavily, it was still to be a routine surgery. The medication she had been taking was ketoconazole due to the disease becoming systemic.

During the operation, Teresa-Rose flatlined. Her heart had stopped. It was now up to the doctors and nurses in the operating room, people she had known having had many medical appointments in Phoenix, to do the work with the proper expertise and tools to resuscitate her. And time was of the essence. The longer the heart stopped and no oxygen entered the brain, the result soon could be permanent brain damage or worse…terminal.

CPR must be started within two minutes. If delayed more than three minutes, the lack of blood to the brain could lead to brain injury. They only had approximately five minutes, ten at the most. Even though the medical team worked on Teresa longer, the survival rate was considered low. If the heart did resuscitate, the brain damage caused by the amount of time without oxygen would put the patient in a needed coma.

Teresa-Rose Earp was declared dead, not after five minutes, but after a full three hours and twenty minutes. The sheet covering her waist down to her feet was unraveled and spread to her head covering her body. The doctors and nurses had faces dripping with sweat as tears ran down their noses, into the surgical masks, and down their operating gowns.

This individual had become a friend of the staff due to the dozens of appointments she had at the hospital in Phoenix. Also, knowing she was an ER nurse and OR nurse anesthetist, Teresa was considered a member of the medical family. This was difficult for all of them.

When the doctor signaled that it was time to call it, everyone in the operating room was emotionally drained. They stood motionless, not understanding what went wrong. It should have been routine. They checked and double-checked everything they did to make sure it was by the book.

A colleague, one of their own, was gone. No one thought, *Why, dear Lord Jesus Christ, oh, why?* They were not believers. They were medical personnel who believed in the power of their education and expertise. The Lord Jesus Christ had nothing to do with this.

Teresa-Rose Earp is still a wonderful person and a beautiful soul. She now lives in Northern Virginia. After an incredible three hours and twenty minutes having been declared dead, her heart began beating.

A miracle? Yes!

Not only is this her story, but it is also her spiritual journey of meeting and rediscovering her life with the Lord Jesus Christ.

CHAPTER 1

Teresa was having difficulty taking in full breaths of air. Her inhalations were interrupted to the point where she felt she needed to cough, and additional air could be taken into her lungs before coughing again. This had been going on for some time now.

She thought again. This was going on not just for some time but on and off for years. She knew her illness would *eventually* become worse. However, *eventually* was not sometime in the future. It was now. And now was not a casual reminder of her illness. It was consistent and sometimes violent from within.

Her body would jerk each time she coughed. The pain in her head would begin to throb as she felt the pressure building with each new cough. Coughing relieved the pain, but Teresa knew another episode of coughs would return. With it came additional moments of pressure on her head.

Her nose was not running, and she did not feel like she had a temperature. Then again, at this particular moment, she had not taken her temperature, so she really couldn't determine if it was elevated. She did feel a lot of aching throughout her entire body. She often experienced chills where the shaking inside her felt like all of her bones were going to pull apart.

But now she felt like coughing more than just a few coughs, stopping, and then coughing again, all while trying to inhale fully. She was having trouble catching her breath. The air entering her lungs did not fully compensate for her body's needs.

Teresa put the small two-month-old infant she was holding and feeding with breast milk from La Leche League in her crib. After giving birth, Teresa was unable to breastfeed due to the medication she had been on for her disease. The baby refused formula from a bottle. If it wasn't breast milk, it was nothing, and that was not an option.

Thank God for the La Leche League. They provided an ample supply of breast milk and sent word throughout the area and other chapters that a great deal of milk was needed. A premature baby had been born. The mother was on multiple medications and unable to breastfeed her child.

Teresa rushed into the bathroom and felt the cough about to explode from her mouth. This time, however, she grabbed for a tissue, instead of using her hand to cover her mouth, and coughed deeply. Feeling the liquid coming out of her mouth and knowing it went into the tissue, she pulled her hand and tissue away from her mouth. She glared into the tissue and saw the many droplets of blood. Then she felt it again.

Reaching to grab another tissue, she coughed again, but more deeply and violently. The thrust from the cough pulled her head backward and then jerked forward. The stream came out of her mouth as she then covered the tissue to prevent it from falling out of her hand and into the sink.

She gazed again into the tissue and hoped part of her throat had not been coughed up. Little tidbits could be seen within the blood. Maybe even floating pieces of muscle? No way! This was not a scene from a horror film where a space villain shoots out. Pulling her hand away again and lowering it to the counter with the tissue still in her hand, she glared into the tissue and eyed the deep-red liquid. It was thick, gooey, and all-telling in her mind. No space villain though. However, things were getting worse.

No, things were not getting worse. Worse was a few days ago, a week ago, when the coughing was not as severe. Worse was when coughing was coughing, and no blood exploded out. This was full hemoptysis, a medical term she had been prepared for after listening to her doctor and knowing, as an OR nurse working in the ER area with full knowledge, that the medication had not worked in the past and was not working now.

The reason she had to stop taking her medication in the first place was because she was pregnant. The medication was not good for the fetus. It was surely not working now because the disease was no longer rapidly increasing in her left lung. It was now fully enveloping the lung, and deep inside, she knew—she knew in her mind that her life could not continue in a normal manner. She knew, as the nurse she was, that this episode was no longer tolerable daily. It was not tolerable on an hourly basis. Still, she knew, in her heart, that she was not ready to accept what was about to occur.

Was it time to rush to the hospital? Again? Did she really believe that she needed to get her husband away from work to drive the long distance? Again? Did she want to notify her sisters and brother that this was now an emergency and could be life-threatening?

AGAIN?

It was no longer a matter of "could be" life-threatening. It WAS life-threatening. Her medical history demanded that she react now, not later. Her instincts as a medical professional required her to move quickly and professionally with the thought that not only a patient's life was in jeopardy, but also it was her life.

Then she felt it again. Only this time, she did not reach for a tissue. She lowered her head into the sink and coughed a half dozen times and then took another quick breath six more times. Teresa kept coughing while gasping to get some air and felt the blood and mucus spurting out and slowly dripping into the drain. Her head began to cloud, and she felt dizzy. She was holding onto the sides of the sink for dear life. Her hands became white from the pressure and tightness of holding onto the sink.

Please, dear Lord Jesus, she thought. *Please help me.* There was one other problem to be worried about. Teresa didn't need to remember she had just given birth to her third child, who was two months premature. The very first time she coughed up blood, she found out that she was four and a half months along after having an ultrasound. Now believing she was pregnant, the coughing may have been due to the pregnancy. She needed to stop imagining things and come back to reality. The pregnancy did not cause the coughing. Her disease was on and off for years. The pregnancy was a blessing. It was not a hindrance. The pregnancy would bring a new life into the world.

This was a blessing from God and Jesus Christ. It was not an interruption from the disease she had been fighting for some time. *So come back to the present time and stop the misconceptions, the excuses, and ill-conceived contradictions and MOVE!* Joey was in her crib. Teresa did not hear her crying and believed she was okay. She just put her down. Why was she worried?

Teresa was worried because she was a two-month-old baby. That's why! And she also had two other young children, which meant her sister needed to be called so she could watch them while her husband drove her, AGAIN, to the hospital. Later, she admitted to herself that her conclusions for coughing were out of whack. She knew what was going on inside of her. She understood the disease that was slowly progressing within her. There were many doctor appointments and many tests. She realized that she was not ignorant of the facts and that her education and knowledge as a nurse couldn't turn away the ultimate results and truths.

When the violent coughing had ceased, she raised her head and felt the throbbing in her temples. She lost her balance for just a short moment and then caught herself holding onto the sides of the sink. The slight dizziness subsided, and her eyes focused.

When she was seven months pregnant, she knew that the coughing could be affecting the baby, and she needed to rush to the hospital. And when her beautiful child was born, everything was okay. Her baby girl, although premature, was not showing any signs that Teresa's illness had caused damage to the fetus. Joey would grow up to be a beautiful woman.

Now it was repeating. Only this time it was not just worse. It was becoming catastrophic in her mind. Teresa gazed into the mirror and quickly thought, *How long? When did it begin? Why me?* She thought about the beginning of her life back in New York. Her eyes became hazy and blurred again. She held onto the sink once again afraid that she might fall.

CHAPTER 2

Teresa-Rose was born on February 2, 1961, in Brooklyn, New York, on the day of the Presentation of the Lord, with a veil over her head. In medical terms, this meant that she was born inside a completely intact amniotic sac. Essentially, the water bag never broke.

At some point during the pregnancy, the water bag was supposed to break. This would signal that it was time to go to the hospital and deliver the baby. For labor to progress to the point where the water wouldn't break on its own was considered very rare. It looked as if the baby was born in a thin, see-through sac with amniotic fluid inside. Another analogy was like that of a very large bubble with fluid inside.

Spiritually, this represented a different explanation. Caul bearers, as they were also sometimes referred to in medical terms, were believed to be quite special. They were said to possess incredible sensitivities and have the ability to navigate and travel through many worlds. Other traits also included seeing the future, having natural healing abilities or being healers, and having psychic gifts.

Jesus Christ was also born with a veil over his head or caul bearer. It's no wonder Teresa was always considered special. How wonderful to be born with the same distinction as Jesus Christ and on the day of the Presentation of the Lord. Although not the direct daughter of God Almighty, she was of the same rarity as a caul bearer. Truly an honor and miracle of its own. She was truly blessed.

Teresa's father was Frederick Jessberger Jr., Fred as he liked to be called. He was the only son of what Teresa described as a "very mean and stern" Catholic grandmother and a grandfather who was just "being very cross." Both were extremely disciplined, and the rules of the household were to be followed without question. "This is our home, our rules, and they are not to be questioned! Any problems?" No one ever thought to voice any problems, at least not in front of the grandparents.

Fred Junior was also a devout Catholic as the family attended Mass every Sunday at a Latin Mass in Brooklyn. "Serving often" for the sake of the Lord Jesus Christ was paramount to their souls and survival.

Teresa's mother was Jacqueline or Jacquie. Jacquie was Baptist until the age of twenty-one when she converted. She converted to Catholicism before she met Fred Junior. They did meet at work as both were employed by Bell Telephone.

The family first lived with Teresa's grandparents in a brownstone in Brooklyn. Money needed to be saved. Families always shared the personal and structural years of a marital foundation when a young couple was just starting out.

Saving money was a priority for both Fred Junior. and Jacquie. The sooner they could afford their own place, the better. While Teresa's parents were wonderful, kind, and considerate, they knew it would be more harmonious living in their own home.

Fred worked for AT&T as a technician, while Jacquie worked as a phone operator. It was a difficult life back in the forties in the United States with World War II affecting everyone. Families stuck together.

When Teresa was four, the family moved to Brentwood, Long Island. In total, Teresa was one of six children in her family. Michael was born in 1950. Mary was born in 1958 and became a nun on her deathbed, but that was another story. Frederick III, also known as Ricky, was born in 1959. Teresa was the fourth child. Jacqueline Junior, also known as Jacquie, entered the family in 1962. The sixth and final sibling, Jonni-Ann, came into the world in 1967.

Michael was the only grandchild who melted the hearts of Fred's parents. They put aside their disciplined and stern attitudes somewhere else when Michael entered the scene. He received all kinds of toys and gifts that the others weren't even allowed to touch. It was Michael who could do no wrong in their eyes. "God forbid we were to even have fun in the 'historic basement' of my grandparents' home," Teresa explained. It was filled with Michael's toys. No wonder he wanted to visit them often.

Teresa was very outgoing while growing up on Long Island. Slender in stature and with long, light-brown hair, her hazel eyes stood out as they were wide and always appeared to be searching. Maybe this was attributed to her birth, but Teresa was constantly asking questions and wanting to know as much as possible. Her ability to remember every incident spoken and explained to her was incredible.

It was as if there was an encyclopedia inside her head. It was also rare to contradict the one who remembered everything, every incident, every book ever read, and every conversation. The only one who would win an argument within the household was Teresa—not that there were many arguments. Just the run-of-the-mill American family if one wanted to present their observation of the "run-of-the-mill American family" in the 1960s.

In the '60s, Long Island was a great place to bring up any family. After World War II and post Korean War, many families from the city moved eastward to the suburbs of New York City. It was less congested. Housing back then was less expensive, and a person could take the train into the city or drive the Long Island Expressway ending at the Queens–Midtown Tunnel.

Teresa's mother played the piano and organ. Performing music in church was like being in a heavenly band. Not only was Jacquie a good organist but she was also truly gifted. She could play any song at any time without having to practice. In fact, Jacquie required all her children to either sing in the chorus or play an instrument. Michael eventually had a rock-and-roll band. However, that was later during his teens and early twenties in New York.

Teresa's oldest sister, Mary, played guitar. Jacquie Junior played the clarinet. Teresa took up the flute after learning the tonette in second grade. Everyone learned the tonette in grade school back in the 1960s. It was a simple instrument. Teresa just mastered it quickly and needed a real instrument that didn't sound plastic even though the tonette was plastic.

As stated, singing was a part of the entire family. Spiritual music rang out in joy every week. The smile on Teresa's mother beamed with pride. It was all for the glory of Jesus Christ.

CHAPTER 3

Life was going pretty good until Fred Junior decided to transfer from AT&T to Contel in California. It was specifically in Central California and Kern County. It was not Hollywood or the beaches as Teresa and her siblings knew from watching the television.

Kern County included the cities of Bakersfield and Ridgecrest just south of the Sequoia National Forest. Needless to say, these were and still are considered desert communities. There may not have been as many people as on Long Island, but Kern County was also growing and needed many trained, technical individuals.

So it was "California Here We Come," whether the family agreed or not. They had no choice. Fred, being the head of the household and breadwinner, had the final say.

Unfortunately for Jacquie and the children, Fred left for California before them. This meant as soon as he could get the first plane to the West Coast and his new job. The sooner he got there, the quicker the paychecks would begin. This left Jacquie in charge of selling the house and moving the family to the central desert neighborhood of Inyokern in the city of Kern. This was more than a chore.

This was difficult as Jacquie paid the bills and had her siblings and the children help with cleaning and packing up the house. Then they loaded everything they could to travel safely and feel secure along the way.

It took six months to accomplish this huge task before leaving Long Island for the long trip to the Golden State. Teresa was just six at that time and in second grade. The good news for the family was that her grandmother, her father's mom, traveled to California with them. Another adult certainly was a big help not only with the move but also with watching the younger children.

Settling in Inyokern after the long trip, unpacking everything, and getting to know the area was short-lived. After only a year and a half, the family packed everything up again and moved to Garnerville, Nevada. This was a small city that was thirty miles outside of Carson City, the capital of Nevada.

Today, Garnerville was considered an excellent community for retirees and people who work from home. Against a backdrop of snowcapped Sierras, Garnerville was also the home of many Danish immigrants who had originally arrived in 1870. Their relatives still lived in Garnerville. Unique stores, saloons, and eateries lined the streets of this quiet town.

Back in the 1960s, Garnerville was considered a sleepy town. There were a few who wanted to build it up with subdivisions. Homes, better water, sewer service, and electricity were annexed to the District of Garnerville. Within what was called Unit 1 of the Garnerville Ranchos General Improvement District, there were many districts proposed at that time. Inside the districts were many units. Inside the units were many successes and many failures.

Garnerville was promoted as a growing community away from the capital city of Nevada. The telephone company was also growing as Fred requested the transfer, and the phone company paid for it. Since Fred and Jacquie were employees of the phone company, moving the family was relatively easy.

The family was there for two years. Jacquie hated it. Fred loved it as he grew fond of the slots in Carson City. Realizing it was only thirty miles from their home, Fred could spend all night long playing nickel slots. All night long was not an exaggeration. One might believe that playing nickel slots couldn't be too expensive. After all, it wasn't dollar slots or poker. A nickel? Come on! How much could a person lose at the nickel slots?

Let's just say that after two terrible years, Jacquie requested a transfer back to California for both of them with Fred's eventual cowered consent. The phone company complied, and the family was moved to Ridgecrest, California, not far from Inyokern where they had been.

Teresa was in fourth and fifth grades in Garnerville, Nevada. Nothing like getting to know the area and almost fully adapting to the new city. There were new schools, new friends, "etcetera, etcetera," as Yul Brenner would say. The good news for Teresa was that she no longer played the tonette but was playing the flute. She accomplished this while in Nevada. Teresa wasn't just average. She was really good. Her mother was teaching her, and she played beautifully.

Did anyone really believe that she would be just average? Teresa was never average in anything. She also was an excellent sight reader of music. It would soon become an apparent positive for her at her young age.

Then it was moving out again. The US school system in the 1950s, 1960s, and 1970s was elementary school (kindergarten through sixth grades), junior high school (seventh to ninth grades), and senior high school (tenth to twelfth grades). The changes in the school system throughout the United States didn't take effect until the late 1980s.

In sixth grade, Teresa went to a charter school at China Lake Weapons Center, just ten minutes north of Ridgecrest. According to her brother Ricky (or Frederick III), it was a school for "brainiacs." Teresa was definitely a gifted student with excellent grades.

Because Teresa's mother would also school her children once they got home, their level of success in their prospective grades exceeded that of the other students. Teresa, on the other hand, was reaching an even higher level. She needed more challenges to keep her mind ahead of the curve. She needed the gifted school at China Lake Weapons Center for that added push and influence. She was learning in classes that weren't taught if she had stayed in a regular elementary school classroom in the sixth grade. The one thing all parents wanted for their children was to not get bored in school.

The family still played their musical instruments and sang. Jacquie kept up with the piano and organ and would play in any church whenever she could. The gift of music was from Jesus Christ. She was never going to stop rejoicing and giving back for these gifts. She knew this made God Almighty and Jesus Christ pleased and always gave that credit to them. Going to church was relatively simple. There were many churches in the Central Valley of California. There were many denominations of churches. Naturally, Catholicism was their preference. Mass was something her parents loved and wanted to continue when they were in California. There was just one problem. There were no Latin Masses.

"What have they done with the church?" was all her father would say. It was too liberal for him. Without a Latin Mass, things just didn't meld properly for Fred. Due to this unforgivable state, life became unfortunate as the ritual of Mass every Sunday soon became a thing of the past. However, Jacquie knew that playing the organ, wherever she could and in whatever house belonged to the Lord, would eventually result in the promises of the Lord. She was playing Jesus's music. She was silently converting everyone to Catholicism without them even knowing the music was from the Catholic Church. It was glorious, harmonious, and spiritually lifting the souls of all the parishioners.

Teresa's gifted school at the China Lake Weapons Center? That lasted for only a year as Fred was on the move again. Teresa loved going to that school. It gave her the opportunity to learn more than she would have had at a secondary elementary school. They pushed her to strive higher at CLWC.

Now approaching seventh grade, the family, with the help and service of the phone company, packed up the household goods and furniture, packed up all the personal belongings, and relocated to Barstow, California. This was sixty-two miles southeast of Ridgecrest and off I-15. This would be their new home city. In her mind, Teresa was thinking it wouldn't last. She wondered if, and when, her father and mother would uproot the family a fifth time.

CHAPTER 4

Barstow was a larger city that also intersected with I-40 to the east. This interstate was built to eventually allow travelers to drive from Barstow, California, to Wilmington, North Carolina. Although the entire I-40 would not be completed for decades, in 1975, the I-40 was completed from Barstow to Needles, Arizona. It was also a major trucking stop as I-15 was completed in 1966 for a nonstop drive to Las Vegas.

So with Las Vegas to the northeast and Needles to the east, Barstow was definitely *the* city for growth, work, and education. In addition to being a major trucking stop, Barstow was also a major railroad hub. This brought in a great deal of merchandise from the east. Unload the trains and load their contents onto the trucks, and voila! Railroad and interstate transportation flourished.

One would like to believe that after more than a few moves, a family would settle down. They would relax and realize careers would last in one location. Schools could be completed to graduation. This was what finally occurred. Fred worked as a toll test board tech at the phone company. Jackie was an inside installer repairman also with Contel. Repair person was not yet the term used until very late in the twentieth and early twenty-first centuries.

Living in the desert town of Barstow, in the Mohave Desert of San Bernardino County, California, was not as easy as many city people would believe. There wasn't the terminal bumper-to-bumper traffic that was experienced every hour of every day in Los Angeles. It was faster than Ridgecrest, where they once lived. It was definitely busier than Garnerville, Nevada, and there weren't slot machines nearby.

The hustle and bustle of a major metropolis was not felt in Barstow regularly. Like any city, it did have its pros and cons. It was quieter even though there were many trucks for interstate transportation. Even the noises from the railroads didn't disturb the rural–suburban feel.

However, I-15 was and is actually a miserable drive going to Las Vegas and back during the holidays. Whenever there was a long weekend from Friday to Sunday, expect delays. If it was a longer holiday weekend from Friday to Monday, forget even thinking about the ease it would take getting to Las Vegas and returning. An extra day of gambling in Las Vegas was worth it.

People from Los Angeles and, in fact, all the surrounding neighborhoods, which basically meant everybody, loved and still loves to travel early and try to beat the existential traffic that would pile up along I-15. Heaven help them if there is also a traffic accident along the way. It could take up to double the amount of time.

Businesses expanded and brought in more hotels. Then there were more fast-food restaurants and gas stations. For many, Barstow was and is a good medium-sized city to stop and get a meal before driving the balance of miles to Las Vegas. Even the tour buses would make stops in Barstow. Whether they originated in Los Angeles or from the beaches of Santa Monica, the distance of one and a half to two hours to Barstow broke up the long ride. A late lunch or early dinner could be purchased at many of the fast-food or food mall locations.

Then there were the beer purchases. On a tour bus, a person could become quite intoxicated well before reaching Las Vegas to the north or Laughlin to the east. Loud, raucous voices singing or dancing in the aisles had occurred many times.

In Bartow, one could also explore some of the local areas of interest. Along California State Route 58, Barstow was, and still is, the home for many Indian tribes. This included the Paiute-, Serrano-, and Shoshonean-speaking bands. Travelers would stop and peruse the small shops and learn the history along the way.

There was also the old Calico Ghost Town to the north, about fifteen to thirty minutes from downtown Barstow. Take the exit off

I-15 and drive a lonely two-lane road to the hills and one would see the abandoned small town of Calico. This was where silver was discovered in 1882. Miners rushed to get in their digs hoping for fortunes. Then in 1883, Borax became a major mining commodity. This brought in even more people as Barstow grew larger.

Los Angeles had the Pacific Ocean to the west and the mountains to the east. Barstow had the desert on both sides. The cost of living in Los Angeles was much higher. Living in Barstow from the 1970s until the 1980s did have many good points, as stated, and the pros outweighed the cons. Housing was much less. Crime was much lower. The time it took to go to another city such as San Bernardino, California, to the southeast or Lake Havasu City, Arizona, to the east was much "smoother" than traveling from downtown Los Angeles to the beaches of Santa Monica.

While it was only fifteen miles from downtown Los Angeles to Santa Monica, it could sometimes take as long as an hour or more in bumper-to-bumper traffic. And life overall was a bit slower in Barstow. When I said "smoother," I meant less traffic. The actual time from Barstow to San Bernardino was approximately one hour and six minutes. A "smooth" drive always felt better than a short stop-and-go trip taking longer than usual.

Barstow was also the closest city to Fort Irwin. This was a very large army facility that "provides realistic joint and combined arms training." Fort Irwin was the first exit north from the outskirts of Barstow when traveling on the I-15. Take that exit and it was another twenty-six miles west on a lonely one-lane in either direction and sometimes expanded to add a passing lane for faster vehicles.

Many soldiers take their leaves traveling to Las Vegas for long weekends. However, evenings could be spent in Barstow at one of the many restaurants, bars, and hotels. Although there were frequent signs along the trip from Barstow to Fort Irwin warning motorists to stay awake and be alert, there were quite a few crosses on the side of the road. This indicated the area where accidents, deaths, and dates of accidents occurred. At last count in 1988, there were at least thirty-five. That was more than one for every mile from the exit off I-15 to the entrance of Fort Irwin.

Why mention Fort Irwin and the road? It was just one example of the dust that could be tossed up into the air when cars traveled at more than a hundred miles an hour and thrown for miles. Another was the dust storms that came with the Santa Ana winds, making I-15 a very dangerous interstate.

As it had occurred in the past, visibility could drop precipitously. Santa Ana winds were not just a seasonal occasion. They occurred quite frequently during the year in the central and southern California areas. If one were to drive with their windows down, the dust swallowed up by that unprepared driver would eventually cause breathing and lung problems. This was an eventual issue for Teresa.

With Fred and Jacquie now employed at Contel and secure with their employment status, Teresa and her siblings attended their prospective schools and did all the things that they enjoyed as children and teens. Moving was now considered a thing of the past.

During the entire time that Teresa lived in Barstow with her parents, she would get sick. There would be a lot of coughing. She had to drive from one desert town to another over many years due to work. There were numerous hours spent in her car with the windows down. Her unsuspecting lungs inhaled a great deal of outside air. Along with the smoggy air were many particles of dust, toxic dust, dust that carried the disease that would eventually cause her years of problems.

CHAPTER 5

Teresa was now moving up to high school and tenth grade. Her accomplishments included playing in the band in junior high. Already quite adept at sight reading, this was a huge plus for Teresa when playing the flute. The band instructor was quite impressed.

She had heard of a prestigious orchestra within the United States called America's Youth in Concert. It originally was conceived and began in 1972. It was a division within the Universal Academy. Auditions were held throughout the United States. There would be a band, an orchestra, and a choral group. For Teresa, her audition would be in Los Angeles.

What was happening in the early 1970s was exceptional if one were to live at that time. America's Youth in Concert was one of the extraordinary concepts and opportunities for young people. It was a time of great change and political unrest. The war in Vietnam was raging. President Nixon had resigned because of Watergate. There was too much turmoil for any generation.

It's ironic that most of today's young generation didn't even know what a telephone booth was or had ever seen one. A phone call would only cost a dime. Some of the phones were originally rotary. New phones in the booths were touchtone.

A person could buy a new car for under $2,500. Gasoline was only fifty-five cents per gallon. At one point, gas was rationed out in odd and even days. Your license plate designated what day gas could be purchased.

Teresa explained that she once wrote a letter to President Carter regarding the gasoline lines. While hoping to receive an explanation or some sort of reply, nothing ever arrived. Needless to say, this was one of the many huge embarrassments for President Carter. The

Cold War put immense pressure on the US school system as math and science were pushed on every student. Even with the need for these important subjects, music, physical education, driver's education, and even typing classes were all required. Students needed and were expected to be well-rounded.

It was 1976, and Teresa was sixteen. Her audition for America's Youth in Concert was at UCLA in Westwood, California. Her mother drove her, and it would take almost two hours from Barstow. When they got there, a quick restroom stop, and off they were to the audition area.

Needless to say, it went without a hitch. Teresa's pitch was perfect. Not one flat or sharp note was played. She was basically flawless. After what she deemed was a long wait, she had succeeded in becoming a part of this large, exceptional group of talented young American musicians. She was chosen to be a part of the band and in the first flute position even though there were only two flutists.

Rehearsals were to be held at Rider's College in New York. Her family pooled together the resources needed. Room and board, meaning all hotels and meals, would be provided. This was actually a misnomer because the hotels would be, for the most part, on college campuses. Food wasn't in restaurants but in cafeterias on the campuses. However, anything outside of the itinerary would be considered extras, and costs were to be covered by the individual musician. This included souvenirs, snacks, etc. Side trips, if taken, were to be on a prenotification schedule. The performance schedule was tight. Moving from city to city and country to country was well prepared in advance. That's not to say they didn't have their free time. All work and no play was not the mantra since those in charge knew that this was a once-in-a-lifetime opportunity for most. They would also experience more than just performing in different halls, theaters, and auditoriums.

The rehearsal schedule would last an unbelievably short amount of time before they were off to play in Philadelphia in front of the Liberty Bell. It was amazing to hear the music being played without errors. These young people were the best in their fields and schools.

Thousands auditioned. Nine hundred would be chosen for all three groups.

Everyone would be closely chaperoned since no one was to think about getting out of line or into trouble. They were representing their schools, towns, or cities, and their families would be watching. Their political representatives would be watching. Their country would be watching. And yes, it was televised. Newspaper articles were written daily since the itinerary included visiting many countries and dignitaries. Imagine the spotlight on nine hundred students, the directors of this wonderful company, chaperones, and tour guides. It was immense.

It should be noted that America's Youth in Concert lasted almost a year. The band would play during the summer months. The orchestra and choral groups were scheduled at different months of the year. Each group was impressive, but nine hundred youths were not all traveling at the same time.

After playing at the Liberty Bell, the group was off to play at Carnegie Hall. Carnegie Hall was, and is, considered one of the most prestigious venues throughout the world. Professional musicians, artists, actors, and comedians dreamed of performing at Carnegie. It was thought to be the pinnacle of one's career to have this beautiful hall on one's resume.

Step into Carnegie Hall before the audiences arrive, and the immensity of the lights burning throughout the theatre would reveal an awesome spectacle. The chairs were covered in rich red velvet. The carpets matched the color of the chairs in the same crimson red. The walls were painted in gold and white. When the thousands of lights were turned down to view an empty hall and stage, it literally could take one's breath away.

Walk up to the top of the balcony and sit in the last row, and opera glasses would be required if one would want to know what the facial expressions of the performers were showing. Even the top row of the audience changes when every seat in the hall was occupied. The roar and echo of a resounding, cheering crowd would explode with approvals and applause.

The empty stage could appear to be so lonely if only a large piano were positioned in the center. However, should a virtuoso pianist strike the keys on that piano, the instrument would magically transform the stage into a brilliant musical phenomenon. The loneliness would obviously disappear.

Everything within Carnegie Hall would become a vision when the lights were turned down. The audience would hold their breath as the curtain, if closed, was raised. The concert would begin. Magic was about to occur. Put a full band or orchestra of talented young musicians on the stage, and eyes would light up. Not only were the smiles of these musicians beaming as they were proud to have been chosen to represent all of America, but also the performances they gave reassured everyone of the choices that they made to get to this point. With the hall lights turned low, the stage showed an image of light from behind the curtain. One could hear the rustling of the members walking to their chairs.

Teresa walked onto the stage and took her seat amongst her peers. All of the performers grasped their instruments and waited. The curtain was brought up. The band appeared and was still. The conductor entered from behind the side of the curtains and took his place on the podium. Once his hands were raised, everyone prepared to strike the first note on their instruments. With the first down stroke of the conductor's hands, music was heard as Carnegie Hall lit up. It would be an evening of true, remarkable rapture. It would consist of different genres and styles of music. It would amaze and strike the audience of every state of the United States to bring them to a standing ovation. The reviews would be nothing short of an overwhelming success.

Part of the tour included playing before Queen Elizabeth of England at the Royal Albert Hall. Located in the city of Westminster, it was considered London's most iconic venue. The architecture was in the style of Italian Renaissance. It was opened in 1871 and hosted more than three hundred events each year. From the outside view, it was described as an elliptical form. The inside was circular and had an awesome, beautiful view from any seat from bottom to top.

Imagine the roar of the crowd echoing after the concert was completed. The hairs on all the arms of the performers would stand up to mimic the applause of the crowd. The conductor instructed the band to take another bow and the audience wanted more. It was truly another accolade for every American youth. In front of the Eiffel Tower in Paris, the crowds were inspired. Teresa was in Innsbruck, Austria. The tour continued to include Rome, Florence, and Venice in Italy. Trips to Ireland, Scotland, and countless other beautiful lands that people only dream of visiting were part of an itinerary that was as magical as any imagination.

It was the first time Teresa had been away from her family. Although she was technically by herself, this family included new friends, acquaintances, and places everyone wanted to visit. It would only go on for as long as a summer tour, but the memories lasted a lifetime.

The final concert was back at Carnegie Hall. This would be their final act to a glorious experience. According to Teresa, it was so much better than the first time they played.

And why wouldn't it be better? They began with their second performance at Carnegie Hall. They were still getting used to their new positions within the group. Although they would be deemed perfect the first time, any mistakes that might have, or might not have, been heard were gone. They were now all used to the excellence of their "sound."

As actors in a musical production on Broadway, each inspired the other to be better. Each fed off the characters they played but knew to reciprocate and anticipate each coming line. Each action had a reaction that filled the stage with moments of incredible feelings.

It's like being in heaven or as many would believe heaven to be and have heard. There's nothing bad. There's only good. There's only the beauty that surrounded your soul to be near with Jesus Christ.

For Teresa and everyone who performed with the large group, this was their heaven on earth. The feeling of success and accomplishment was beyond anything they had experienced for a long time. They were all young and felt they were impervious to failure. Their futures were shining bright.

Although Teresa had made many friends within the group, none of them truly lasted. It was a few summer months of stars shining within the souls of each band member. Who truly remembers all of those you meet during one specific summer? It's like going to summer camp and being close to your cabinmates. Do you remember any of the names? All you do remember are the good days and memories of fun.

There was a reunion ten years later in Los Angeles. Teresa did attend. However, there were many who did not attend. As with any reunion, name tags were provided. The afternoon was cordial and polite. It was the only reunion Teresa would attend.

CHAPTER 6

Teresa met Timothy, or Tim as he preferred, while in high school. Tim was a tennis player. Tall, slender, good-looking with an infectious smile, a full head of thick, brown hair, and dark-brown eyes, he was everything a high school girl would want in a date or relationship. He was two years older than Teresa, a junior, and she was a freshman. Teresa did graduate high school one year early as her grades excelled due to her "brainiac" mind.

As with any relationship, high school, college, or others, Teresa and Tim were inseparable. They went everywhere together. He had his tennis matches where she could root for Tim. He would drive Teresa to her nurse's aide job after school at Rimrock Nursing Home in Barstow. Her love of working with the medical staff and helping others were the reasons she went to nursing school after high school.

While in Florence, Italy, during that magical tour, Teresa did one thing for herself and Tim. She knew Tim was the person she wanted. She felt she could not live without him for the rest of her life. She walked to the Jewelry Bridge in Florence and purchased two twenty-four-karat wedding bands. It was technically a gift from Teresa's mother as she had provided the spending money to last the summer.

Tim and Teresa married. They decided to marry while Teresa was still in high school. She was seventeen and very much in love. They would start having a family after Teresa received her nursing degree in two years.

Teresa worked in the city of Lancaster at Antelope Valley Hospital Medical Center in the ICU and other facilities for over ten years. The distance from her home to the hospital was over an hour by car. Again, the driving was the desert areas only. Route 58 from

Barstow to Lancaster was preferred. It was faster and took less time if one would decide to take local roads.

Teresa met Yolanda while in nursing school. She was a black woman, 5'3" in stature, who greased her hair and adorned a shower cap on her head when she drove on back roads and old State Route 58. Since they both worked at the same hospital, they had tons of conversations that included personal lives like boyfriends and family. They also joked and loved to laugh.

"Okay, girlfriend," Teresa would joke. "What's with the shower cap? You're supposed to leave the shower behind you."

"Have you seen my hair?" Yolanda would explain. "It's thick—thicker than wool when wet. You think I want this blowing in the wind? I also need to keep it from getting too much sun."

Teresa was laughing when she heard this. At first she couldn't think of a thing to say. The actual reason Yolanda wore the shower cap was to moisturize her hair. She had her hair tightly coiled with lard.

After a few months with Teresa driving to work and Yolanda in the passenger seat, Teresa noticed that inside the roof of the car where Yolanda sat was showing a large spot. It became a funny, continuous joke about how large the spot would grow. Sometimes, Yolanda would forget to wear the shower cap. Yolanda's hair was of a tight Afro style. If she didn't wear the cap, she would bounce up and down as they drove the sometimes-bumpy roads. They both tried to clean the spot, but it never came out. Still, their personal joke continued.

The two of them loved their school and their jobs. It was Teresa who excelled faster and moved up to begin working in the ICU. Teresa moved quicker and showed greater promise with the nursing chores as anyone would who possessed that intelligent mind. She remembered everything. Although Yolanda longed for a promotion, she loved working the floor.

A few times when they were driving to work, Yolanda noticed Teresa's coughing was getting worse. She relied on Teresa to do her due diligence and study up on her disease. She would mention it frequently to Teresa.

"Girl!" Yolanda would sometimes say as a joke. "When you gonna get that cough taken care of? You keep coughing and whooping as if you can't even breathe."

"I'm working on it, Yolanda," Teresa would say, hoping nothing more would be added to the conversation.

"You know it's worse than both of us believed at first. Please get it taken care of and see someone. Does it affect you at work?"

"All the time," Teresa would say and laugh. "I gotta get people to notice me so I don't disappear into the woodwork. You know I'm only five feet three."

"It's not the woodwork I'm concerned with, honeybunch," Yolanda would say.

"It's you. Besides, I never look down on you. I'm always looking up to you. You move fast, and you know what the doctor ordered before the doctor even ordered anything. I don't know how you do it."

"It's in my jeans," Teresa explained and pointed to her scrubs and then laughed.

"Let's move on."

Eventually, Route 58, which was only a one-lane highway in both directions, was expanded to accommodate two lanes in both directions. With the population growth in California and the need for less traffic due to the many trucks along the highways, expanding highways and roads was a necessity. It also decreased the amount of time driving from Barstow to Lancaster. It was safer as motorists hated being behind a big rig on old Route 58 and trying to pass.

After they married, Tim and Teresa had two children during their time in Barstow. Autumn was the oldest. Timothy II was the second. A couple of years after Autumn was born, problems began with Teresa and Tim. He became abusive. While it could have been because Teresa was showing signs of great success in her nursing career, Tim was moving slower in the opposite direction. His career stifled him and he wanted changes. Maybe it was male ego. Probably it was not only ego but also pride and jealousy. Tim always wanted to be an employee with the San Bernardino County Sheriff's

Department. He just couldn't pass the tests. His dreams were dying a slow death.

Teresa did admit to not being faithful after Autumn turned two until the time she became pregnant with their son, Timothy II. The abuse Tim was giving Teresa was becoming a problem and a reason she was unfaithful. What woman in their right mind would want to be abused and stay in a marriage? It got to the point where Teresa needed and wanted a separation from Tim.

Having a second child, thus becoming a larger family, was sometimes the reason that people believe marriages would work. As a Catholic, divorce was not the answer—at least not yet! A separation could cause changes in Tim's attitude toward his wife. Hopefully he would feel the love and need for his family and figure out that he had problems and would find a way to solve them. Continually abusing Teresa was definitely not the solution.

Teresa then worked at the San Bernardino Hospital and Medical Center as an OR nurse anesthetist for a few years. Getting to know many doctors and nurses in numerous facilities was also a plus as friendships grew and great trusts were built. She was also developing a wonderful reputation as an OR nurse anesthetist.

Certain doctors always had their special associates and nurses who worked well and could anticipate their moves in the operating room. Teresa knew a great deal of the needs of the doctors who preferred her in the operating room. Thus, she was able to work the shifts of the specialized physicians if they wanted.

This also required more traveling on the dust-filled highways with high winds on I-15. The windows were still lowered while driving. Still, special shifts meant more hours and additional money. Special shifts brought more advantages to the physicians she preferred to work alongside in the operating room.

There was one negative about living and working in these desert cities of California as previously and frequently mentioned. During the summer, the average temperature would be over a hundred degrees. Humidity was low and the air stale. Although the winter weather could drop and average to the high thirties, the dryness in the air sometimes still would exist. This could become a problem if certain precautions were not followed.

Since it was a desert, there was very little rainfall during the year. Air-conditioning was a must in the desert. The coolness of the AC would provide moisture to the lungs and body. While Teresa did have AC in her home, she enjoyed opening her windows so the breeze could be felt at nighttime while saving the costs of high electricity bills each month due to the use of AC. The real reason Teresa drove with the windows down was that she did not have air-conditioning in her car. One of her goals was to eventually purchase a vehicle with AC.

Teresa was treated at San Bernardino County Hospital and Medical Center for coccidioidomycosis. Also known as San Joaquin Valley fever, it was a rare disease. There were fewer than 200,000 cases per year. It was a treatable disease and required a medical diagnosis. The symptoms resembled those of a flu, which included fever, cough, chills, and chest pain.

Only 5 percent to 10 percent of those who got San Joaquin Valley fever would develop serious or long-term problems in their lungs. That represented 10,000 to 20,000 cases. While the medical field would be pleased with that 5 to 10 percent number, the term *only* was arbitrary. In layman's terms, too many were still becoming ill. It could become mind-boggling.

When Teresa was driving with Yolanda for work in Lancaster, she believed this was when she began inhaling the spores that caused her disease. She was also pregnant with her son. This was confirmed when they did a chest X-ray prior to the C-section during the birth of Timothy II.

Since the doctors at the hospital did not know what the results of the X-rays meant, they sent her to San Bernardino County Hospital to do tests. It was then that she was diagnosed. They needed to observe the lesion in her lung. Later the lesion disseminated. It was now diagnosed as systemic coccidioidomycosis. She had nodules on her forearms, little bumps, and she was coughing up blood and lung matter. It was a good sign that it was not muscle being coughed up but still dangerous.

In 1987, Teresa stood at five feet and three inches tall. Her long-dirty blonde hair, as her sister called it, was tied with an elastic band. Her big green (hazel) eyes still dazzled, and she weighed less than a hundred pounds. The impending disease would take a huge toll on her small frame.

As previously stated, Teresa had worked at many medical facilities as an ER nurse. Victor Valley Hospital in Victorville, California, was approximately thirty miles from Barstow. Her shifts were twelve hours on and then twelve hours off for two days with a day in between. As good as the money was with the shifts she enjoyed, getting sick was not in the overall equation. Her coughing persisted. Teresa was still separated. She was considered a single parent and would soon give birth to Timothy II.

After Teresa was diagnosed with San Joaquin Valley fever, her employer kept up her "hopeful" progress. Her hours were long and could be stressful. Making sure that one of their own was doing well also assured them that her patients were being treated with the utmost respect and excellent medical care.

As fate would have it, Tim received an offer to work in the Needles Sheriff's Department. Tim knew he wanted to be a police officer. He applied a few times but never received the offer to move forward and complete the training. His father came through for him since he had connections with the Needles Sheriff's Department. He was able to secure Tim a job as a jailer watching the prisoners.

Even though this was not an actual sheriff's deputy position, Tim jumped at the chance. He knew once he was inside, he could eventually apply and move up the ladder. Tim moved into his parents' trailer home in Park Moabi Regional Park. This was in Needles. He did not know how long he would be a jailer before getting into training, but he knew he couldn't last without his family. Tim wanted the support and love from his wife and children. He was the husband, and he felt they should do whatever he wanted.

As Teresa would explain it, Tim basically kidnapped her and the children and drove them to Needles. There was already a house ready to be set up where they would live together as a happy family whether they liked it or not.

Life as a nurse in San Bernardino or Victorville was, obviously, no longer viable. With the family now being hijacked and moving to Needles, the drive time would seem like an eternity. Needles was more than two hours from Barstow where she had lived. It would be even longer to Victorville and then prohibitive to even think about driving to San Bernardino. Needles was on the border of Arizona.

Knowing that nurses were needed practically everywhere in the country, Teresa hoped that Needles would need her services. The medical industry was always in search of qualified nurses. Little did she realize.

CHAPTER 7

Needles, California, was a desert town situated on the Colorado River. It was founded in 1883 as a way station for the Atlantic and Pacific Railroad, now known as the Santa Fe Railroad. It received its name due to a group of "isolated needlelike peaks" across the border from Arizona. Needles was famous for the Needles weather station as it frequently reported the highest daily temperatures recorded in the United States during the summer months should one rule out Death Valley, California, to the northwest. It was considered a "sparse suburban feel," according to a Web site, when inquiring about Needles. Most residents owned their mobile homes. Accepting a new job and moving the family to Needles did not, unfortunately, afford the luxury of ownership as Tim and Teresa soon found out. They were able to rent a two-bedroom, one-bath house.

Needles was also not far from Laughlin, Nevada. It was only twenty minutes. Laughlin was considered a mini Las Vegas with many hotels and casinos adjacent to the Colorado River. In fact, there was a large walkway along the western portion of the Colorado River connecting many of the hotels and casinos.

One could buy their huge margaritas or piña coladas and drink it while perusing shops and enjoying an outdoor spring, summer, or autumn walk. Or a person could rent a Sea-Doo or boat and enjoy traveling up and down the waters of the Colorado River. All in all, it was a great place for tourists with many vehicles traveling I-40. Tim enjoyed his work as a jailer knowing that the opportunity would soon come and he could begin his training as a real deputy. The sheriff's jailer job lasted almost nine months before he finally received the good news. Tim relished the opportunities he had imagined would one day materialize. There would be a good job, a real future, a pension, and a much-improved paycheck. Finally, there would be prestige, respect, and more.

Tim needed to stop dreaming, look at reality, and come down from the clouds. That's not what would be in store for him as a sheriff's deputy. His job, at first, was training in San Bernardino. He would then eventually be assigned to the Glen Helen Rehabilitation Center in Devore, California. Devore was only sixteen miles west of San Bernardino, California, where Teresa had been working as a nurse.

While her husband worked at his job, Teresa noticed it was becoming more difficult to do her job. She now considered her job raising her two children, looking for a nursing position, managing the home, and getting healthy. Being further into the desert for those nine months was also no relief for her disease as it was becoming more difficult to manage.

During the time Teresa first learned that she had coccidioidomycosis, the doctor prescribed ketoconazole, an "antifungal, antiandrogen and antiglucocorticoid medication." It was supposed to prevent the disease from becoming worse. If applied to the skin, it was used for fungal skin infections. When taken by mouth, and was a less preferred method or option, it was only recommended for severe infections when other oral medication could not be used.

She was also told to do an IV with amphotericin B. It was used for the treatment of invasive fungal infections. Both should have been able to not only lessen the coccidioidomycosis disease but also cure it. Her health turned for the worse after she learned that she was pregnant with her third child. When Teresa went for a routine OB-GYN appointment, her gynecologist gave her the good news of the pregnancy. She had another X-ray taken. It showed the cavitation that calcified and was invading more lung tissue. She was cautioned due to the disease, the medication, and the IV.

As an OR nurse, Teresa was very much aware that the pregnancy could cause additional stress on her body. Terminating the pregnancy was not even a thought on her mind for two reasons. The first was her religious beliefs. The second was she wanted another child.

If this was a girl, and she didn't want to know at the early stage, maybe another female child would change the course of her marriage. The abuse would end. Tim had preferred Autumn to Timmy II. This was what his dad would call him.

Even with Tim finally employed in a steady and secure position in the Needles jail, things never returned to those wonderful carefree days when they were in high school. The teenage and early adult experiences were like no other, and Teresa would have to admit these facts. Where did the time go by?

There were no bills to worry about. There was a vehicle for driving your girlfriend to a romantic hideaway for a few hours of unexpected pleasure either in the car or otherwise. There were parents who were not too worried that their children wouldn't be home at a proper hour of the evening.

During the pregnancy, things began to unravel to the point Teresa didn't know if she could make it to term. The aches, the pains, the chills, and the sweating were almost daily incidences. Then there was the coughing up blood, which increased at a faster pace beyond her imagination. At some point, she wondered if the fetus was even being supplied with the proper nutrients required to get to term.

Being an OR nurse was one item that helped a little. She could handle the almost daily needs to take her blood pressure and temperature. She knew what over-the-counter medication could be swallowed without harming her baby if she required additional medication besides the prescribed ketoconazole and amphotericin B. Whatever rest she needed was a bit stressful since she had two small children. At times she had her mom or sister with her. When additional rest was required to lower the aches and pains, you know the story, her family was always there.

The fungus had no reaction to the prescribed medication. In fact, it settled further into her lungs. It cavitated into the left upper lobe. Teresa was developing shortness of breath. Teresa was concerned not only for herself but also for the health of her child, a daughter they would discover after finally doing the ultrasound.

According to Teresa, everything changed. Depression increased dramatically. She had to stop thinking about looking for a position with another hospital or medical center. She couldn't even look for work at a local clinic. She needed to make sure the health of her unborn child wasn't affected by her depression on top of the medication she was prescribed.

While she was pleased that her husband's training would lead to a permanent position as a sheriff's deputy, she felt that not being able to assist with paying the monthly bills increased her depression. Tim's job paid more than what he had made before. However, a sheriff's deputy didn't start at a high salary. It would take a few years to see a drastic change.

What if something were to happen to her husband? What if a call came and she would learn that there had been an accident? Or worse? How could she support herself and her children? No wonder she became depressed. All of life was taking a turn in the wrong direction.

On top of that was the fact that Tim was still treating her with total disrespect. All the changes he was experiencing didn't lead to being a better husband or father. He was becoming more demonstrative. He was the opposite of what he was in high school and more intolerant. Teresa needed him even though she still wanted a separation.

On top of that, these were negative feelings she knew she shouldn't put into her mind. It only exacerbated the problems as she hoped her feelings would not spill out in public and affect the rest of her family. Teresa needed to pull herself together and act as a professional in her private life as she would when she was a nurse attending to her patients.

While living in Needles, California, the closest pulmonologists that specialized in coccidioidomycosis were in Phoenix, Arizona, at St. Joseph's Hospital and Medical Center. She couldn't travel to her previous doctor in San Bernardino. It was too far, and any hour of the day could determine the traffic viability. Riding in a car for a long period of time with her disease and her pregnancy would put too much pressure on the fetus.

The only problem, and there was always an only problem, was that Phoenix was over two hundred miles to the southeast. This would also be a long drive. These hours seemed terminal.

The three states of California, Nevada, and Arizona all border one another within a triangular vortex. The city of Laughlin, Nevada, was closest and to the north of Needles. On the opposite side of the Colorado River, a short drive from Laughlin, Nevada, was Bullhead City, Arizona. This was due north of Phoenix. With Barstow, California, to the west, Nevada to the east, and Arizona being southeast, there weren't too many options.

Laughlin, although only twenty minutes from her home, wasn't a viable alternative. There wasn't a specialist for Teresa since there wasn't a large hospital. A drive to Bullhead City, Arizona, on the opposite side of the Colorado River would only add a few more miles and minutes. It was a quiet small town also with no major medical facilities.

The results were obvious to Teresa. The fact was St. Joseph's Hospital and Medical Center was newer. There were pulmonologists familiar with the disease. This was not only a no-brainer but also the only option she had when dealing with the life-threatening disease overtaking her body.

Phoenix did present its difficulties. It was over a three-hour drive from Needles. If there were any delays on the freeways due to any number of possibilities, the drive would last over four hours.

For an individual with coccidioidomycosis, this was highly dangerous. For an individual with coccidioidomycosis who was also pregnant, coughing up blood with chills, sweating, aches, and everything else Teresa was feeling, this was now more than unbearable. It was life-threatening.

CHAPTER 8

As for driving to Phoenix for his wife's numerous medical appointments, it was often and fast. It made no difference what time of the day Teresa had the appointment. Tim was, believe it or not, always prepared and accommodating to her needs. This was the only positive anomaly in Tim's attitude toward Teresa.

During the three or four dozen times Teresa needed to be in Phoenix, Tim was always with her. At first, he was the perfect husband and father. Empathy for his wife's medical conditions was a priority.

Unfortunately, their marriage lasted only ten years as Tim's abusive "moods" were getting out of control. Maybe it was the numerous times driving to medical appointments that caused him to change. Maybe it was the stress of missing work that caused his attitude of family first to decline since he loved his job and the possibilities they presented in the future.

Actually, it was none of the above. It was Teresa. She wanted a divorce. She needed to be away from Tim. She needed less stress and no abusive man in her life. She needed, no, she required compassion and understanding. Tim was none of these.

When Tim did become a sheriff's deputy and landed at Glen Helen Rehabilitation Center in Devore, California, there was a report of a sex scandal with a minor. It involved five deputies. It not only hit the local newspapers but also became news throughout Los Angeles and beyond.

Tim was named as one of the five deputies. Was this going on while Tim needed to take care of his wife? Thankfully not! Tim had not yet been assigned to Glen Helen and was still assigned to

Needles and in training. It also didn't matter because he was there when Teresa needed him even though they were now separated.

With the separation, Tim changed drastically. He began to ignore his children. Did the scandal exacerbate his attitude to further ignore his children? What was his frame of mind at the time? The bad news was at the time of the scandal, Tim was actually with Autumn and Timmy II. It was one of the few moments he was spending time with them.

*****

Coming out of her dazed state and seeing the blood in the sink brought Teresa to the present. She had relived her entire life in just a few short moments. Her memories brought all the good and the suffering together in what seemed to be hours. In reality, it was just a flash. It was her mind wishing for what could no longer be real. Teresa needed to stop wishing for the past and think of the immediate future.

She was in dire and desperate need to be driven to the hospital. Again, it did not matter what was going on with Tim because Teresa needed him now. He was required to show that he could be there for her support. It did not matter if they did or did not love each other at the time. Even with Teresa having filed for separation and the fact that Tim had kidnapped them to Needles, this was not the time to think about anything else but getting her to the hospital. Although Tim would say that he did love Teresa, it was only after Teresa's surgery and after she was brought home that life became impossible for all. Their third child, a girl named Joey, was born two months premature on January 21, 1983. It was prior to the current moment. With the coccidioidomycosis in full gear, Teresa was unable to breastfeed.

The La Leche League donated breast milk because Joey refused to take a bottle of formula. She was healthy, happy, and well-taken care of no matter what the mental state of the marriage or family was at the time. For now, this was the only plus. Joey was an angel appearing at just the right and the wrong time.

Two months premature was a blessing. The two months that followed were the beginning of the nightmare.

CHAPTER 9

Teresa knew the staff at the St. Joseph's Hospital and Medical Center. She knew those at the front desk who checked a patient in. She knew the staff in the OR area, the nurses, and the doctors. She knew almost everyone who could be involved with her case as this was her procedure as an OR nurse anesthetist.

It was her protocol to get involved as most medical personnel typically want to know as much information as possible about the patients they must care for. They were required to be familiar with the type of procedures each patient would undergo and the postoperative care that was involved. Many also tried to get to know the family members.

One should never presume, or assume, that the best prognosis or procedure wouldn't go awry. There were always different variables that could arise. Doctors and nurses always checked and double-checked their paperwork prior to any operation.

That was why they always asked the patient their name and date of birth multiple times. They also verified the procedure with the patient by making sure they were operating on the right knee and not the left. Or verifying the left shoulder was to be replaced and not the right.

In Teresa's case, it was like treating a member of the family. But first, her third pregnancy was difficult because the coccidioidomycosis became worse. The spores imbedded into the upper left lobe of her lungs and entered the fifth rib on the left. This caused further deterioration. The coughing became worse. The coughing up of blood became heavier.

Her daughter, Joey, was born at Lake Havasu City at a hospital closer to Needles on the other side of the Colorado River, forty-plus miles to the north. She needed to stop the IV medicine because she couldn't breastfeed while on medication. All of this was a vast picture of what was to soon materialize into a deadly nightmare.

It was no longer something that could be set aside with the amphotericin B IV now that she needed to feed Joey with the breast milk from La Leche League. The ketoconazole pills did nothing to alleviate the symptoms, so that was now out. The fungus became systemic.

It wasn't even a normal drive to the Phoenix hospital the day all hell broke loose. It was "Get me to the emergency room so I don't die and leave a husband with three small children and who knew what mental state he was in." It was "drive as fast as you can and pray that the police don't pull you over even if you are a sheriff's deputy in training. Even if you're speeding recklessly as you have to inform them that you believe your wife is dying and requires immediate medical attention. Provide a police escort! Want to see the blood she's coughing up? So please don't ask questions! Just get me to the damn hospital."

Maybe more descriptive words were used at the time, as an additional "as fast as you can" would be added. It was "Say more prayers than we ever have and hope God and Jesus are listening."

Getting to the hospital was one miracle in itself. Getting into the ER area was as normal as physically possible. That's why it was called the ER. That's why they were ready for Teresa before she got to the hospital.

When the car pulled up, Teresa was removed, although with difficulty from the vehicle, and put on a hospital gurney and wheeled in as quickly as possible. While an IV needle would eventually be inserted into her arm and oxygen into her nose, this would occur once they were in the operating room where machines were ready to monitor.

Tim was told to go into the waiting room. Teresa's family was in a second speeding vehicle. They rushed out of their car and followed Tim. Her brothers, Michael and Ricky, and sisters, Mary and Jacqueline, were all told to wait and be patient. Someone would get back with them when the surgery was over. Her youngest sister, Jonni, was watching the children in a hotel room in Phoenix. All had questions that couldn't be answered. Teresa was wheeled in the operating room, the doors closed, and some had tears in their eyes.

Teresa's family was always close. There were never moments of ill will among any of them. Their parents would have none of it. They would always talk, not yell, with one another. When talking was not done, they sang. If they didn't sing, they would go out to eat as a family.

Now was the most difficult time for the family. We've all seen it on numerous television police dramas and Netflix movies, the terminal waiting, the looking at watches and clocks as if time was standing still and wondering if they were working, the reading of the magazines over and over wishing time would move faster, the sitting down then standing and pacing up and down the room, or the groping at the waiting room door thinking they could look through it and hoping to see a doctor, any doctor, but more importantly Teresa's doctor coming through the door with good news.

Small talk wasn't uttered. What was there to talk about? They all knew what was going on. Teresa had kept her family informed of every incident over the years. They all lived with the disease in their hearts and minds as small prayers for their sister were said from time to time.

Why only Teresa? All of them lived in the desert for the same number of years. All of them inhaled the same dust and dirt. How come their bodies could shuffle and fight the disease and not be affected? Their immune system was the same. Wasn't it?

The same house. The same mother and father. The same genes. Why couldn't Teresa fight off the disease when it was first noticed during the pregnancy? About 5 to 10 percent was the only number someone remembered.

The amount of blood being coughed up in the car was much more violent. The severity of the coughs was constant and appeared never-ending. With Teresa trying to catch her breath after each fit and episode, frustrations grew inside the car with Tim.

Her siblings, being in a second car, would have had a blanket wrapped around her when the chills appeared. If she was dripping with sweat, someone would have been there to wipe down her perspiring face. When she needed hydration, another would have handed her a plastic bottle of water. The comfort from her family would have been constant even if they couldn't get her to stop coughing and spitting up blood.

Now in the waiting room, all of them looked at one another wondering what was to become of their sister. They looked at Tim as each tried to comfort him with silent words of hope. After all, what could they say?

They knew what was going on with the marital life of their sister. The verbal abuse and questions of physical abuse were sometimes vocalized. Taking the family out of the house in Barstow and forcing them to move to Needles were unacceptable in their minds. The many moods of Tim were put aside at this moment. And yet no one wanted to say anything that was deemed trite and superficial. They all knew that waiting was the only heart-wrenching ordeal that had to be confronted in the here and now. They couldn't make time go faster to hear the results sooner. Nor could they turn the clock backward to try and avoid this nightmare.

They needed to rely on each other's strength. No amount of coffee, water, or snacks would make the time go faster. Nothing would make a nurse or doctor materialize from the OR with good or bad news. But why was it taking so long?

Please, Lord Jesus Christ! Let it be good news.

"Should we pray?" Jacquie was heard saying.

Lord Jesus Christ? Pray? What?

They weren't devout Catholics at the time. Teresa considered herself ecumenical but not devout. Going to church was something she felt she needed to do but not as a Catholic Christian. Prayers were not said as often as they had been said in the past.

Her mother was definitely praying. Her sisters Mary and Jacquie always said the blessings. Tim would occasionally read aloud from the family bible.

But now?

Growing up was different. Her family attended Mass as devout Catholics every Sunday This was her mother and father's requirement growing up in New York on Long Island. Then it didn't make a difference where they were since they moved often in the early years as a family.

It was later when the Latin Mass was removed by the Second Vatican Council of 1962–1965 that her father refused to attend as a family. In an effort to modernize the Roman Catholic liturgy, this allowed more participation and understanding of the Mass by the congregation. The Latin Mass was essential to Teresa's father.

For Teresa's mother, as long as they attended church, be it Protestant or preferably Catholic, this was the only item on her list on a Sunday morning. Praying to God and the Lord Jesus Christ revitalized her spirit. She wanted her family to know this spirit. Having a personal relationship with Jesus Christ was the means to living a good life and getting to heaven.

Committing a sin, whether venial or mortal, no matter how small was an immediate visit to the confessional. Taking the Lord's name in vain? According to Teresa, this was never done. Otherwise, it could be a quick swat on the behind and another visit to the confessional. The good news was no one ever found out what the outcome would have been.

Heaven help the child who could not respect the value a prayer to Jesus Christ would bring. They were to monitor each other and voice to their parents should any of them step out of line with these requirements of the home. As a result, life with Jesus Christ and God Almighty nourished each moment of their lives. They all felt better.

Eventually, when that day occurred, when her parents would pass away, going to church every Sunday would not be their norm. Praying each day would not be a normal fixture. Saying a rosary? What rosary? They said a prayer every now and then when it felt convenient for the sake of their needs.

Would it even matter now that one of the family members was on an operating table fighting for her life? Her life was in the hands of the doctors and nurses. What could Jesus do now that their sister and Tim's wife could die?

Spiritual togetherness in the home was one thing. True spiritual togetherness and relationships were nurtured not only in the home but also in a house of worship where many would come together to bind each one of its members to God. The more prayed, the better. If the community of their place of spirituality joined in, it was more powerful.

Reaching out to a member of the church you belong could bring real change in the attitudes of the daily life. There were many voices calling out to join in the community and pray for a dying family member. Another group would sit together and pray for the homeless, the hungry, and those serving in the military.

Praying to God and Jesus Christ for peace in the world, saying a daily rosary, a Divine Mercy, or virtually any prayer can structurally change the inside of a human being. Attitudes change. Anger was vanquished, and a serene feeling in the heart and body lifted a mortal soul.

In the realization that a spiritual entity was always a part of their lives, Jesus Christ was always a name that brought warmth, comfort, togetherness, and mutual respect for one another. However, knowing that there was not an everyday offering of prayer and honor also made them question mortality in the present day. After all, what would occur if omitting prayer each day caused a spiritual void within their souls? Would they go to heaven and be with Jesus? Would they go to purgatory or hell? Not being devout, did it make a difference?

For the first time, this was different. This was that outside shot they could not control. No one ever wanted to think about death. Who would want to exist if the morbid topic of death came up in the daily discussion while no one was even close to being considered old? Old was years away. So why think about it?

The only things to think about were the health of their sisters, brothers, spouses, and children. Waiting was only hoping for a positive outcome. They expected to see the nurse or doctor come out from the closed entrance to the OR with not a worried wrinkle protruding from his or her face. They were not expecting to see a morose individual exiting from the only door that led to their loved one.

But why was it taking so long? It was now much longer than they were originally told from Teresa how long she presumed the operation would last. She didn't believe it would take more than a couple of hours at the most. This was much longer. What was happening?

CHAPTER 10

On the opposite side of the door that separated the family was now a family member fighting for her life. She was on the operating table. The nurses and doctors—people she had met and knew after many consultations, appointments, and visits concerning the disease eating through her lungs—were now in total control of her every breath, so to speak. Teresa was still breathing on her own but was being watched closely.

Since Teresa was an OR nurse anesthetist, she already knew what the preparations would be for her, or any patient, going into surgery. The operating staff assessed her condition. This included taking her vital signs, such as blood pressure, heart, pulse, and temperature. They reviewed the symptoms on her chart and looked at the history of her past and present illnesses. It was noted if there were any allergies and all medications she was currently using—this while working feverishly to understand the immediacy of it all.

An IV was inserted into her forearm by the anesthesiologist so as to make sure she would remain unconscious and comfortable throughout the surgery. An oxygen mask was put over her nose and mouth. One nurse laid an extra blanket over her legs to keep her warm.

The machines monitoring her blood pressure, heartbeat, and oxygen levels all pumped out numbers and lines showing different figures with each passing second. The monitor that showed the heartbeat and heart rate also had a beeping sound. One would notice if the sound increased at faster intervals as this would notify the anesthesiologist if the patient required help. This also alerted to the patient's oxygen needs making sure it was at the correct level.

These were what controlled Teresa's life. The hands working on her were specialists in the field. They knew what the procedures were to go through to succeed in beating the disease eating through her lungs. Not only did Teresa require an upper left lobe lobectomy but also she needed a fifth rib resection as the fungus had invaded her rib. It was not known how long Teresa's surgery would last, but everyone was ready to work if it took longer.

This was what occurred every day, in every OR, in the country. Trained and tireless working professionals in the medical field who had taken the Hippocratic Oath to keep people alive moved in precise motions. Nurses listened to the instructions of the lead physician, if there was more than one. Surgical instruments moved from one hand to the other without a missed cue or step. If one nurse's hand was wiping any excess blood with a surgical towel, another was assisting the doctor with the surgical instruments.

All seemed to be going according to plan as they first worked on the fifth rib resection. It was during this procedure that the heart monitor began to beep. The electrocardiogram (ECG) machine was showing erratic movement of the pumping of Teresa's heart.

General anesthesia did have the ability to cause abnormal heart activity. Furthermore, if an arrhythmia, or heart beating faster, already existed due to a precondition, the medical staff would already know to remain vigilant in monitoring the patient's vital signs during surgery.

The doctors and nurses all knew Teresa's history with previous pregnancies and surgeries. They all read and reread the notations from other medical staff who worked on her. They were ready to jump should another complication materialize as they made sure, prior to the surgery, to become as knowledgeable as possible of the disease overtaking her lungs. They were the experts. That's why they were a part of the OR medical staff.

When the heart flatlined, it was called asystole. This was when the heart's electrical system failed thus causing the heart to stop pumping. The heart's electrical activity resembled that of a flat line on the ECG should this happen.

And this was exactly what occurred during the surgery and quickly. No one anticipated it at this time and so early in the surgery. But this was instant and required immediate attention without even thinking. The response was automatic. The reflexes of the medical staff kicked in immediately.

One could analogize it to a massive fire having broken out in a warehouse storing toxic chemicals. Only seconds passing could result in multiple deaths if anyone was inside the warehouse or the surrounding area. Firefighters had seconds to respond by climbing onto the fire trucks. Then they would leave the station and drive to the emergency. Then a few, and only a few, extra minutes would pass setting up on the site and getting out the equipment to analyze and initiate a response before a monumental catastrophe was realized.

Only that analogy lasted longer than what was required in the OR. The doctors and nurses didn't have the extra minutes to set up the equipment. It was right in the operating room. If it took a few extra minutes to respond, a person's life, this being the identity of Teresa-Rose Retzlaff, would expire. The estimated maximum time normally needed to get the patient's heart to start beating again was five minutes. Anything passed that and there could be severe and permanent brain damage due to the oxygen level no longer getting to the brain. Anything passed ten minutes, the chances for the patient to survive were low.

The doctors and nurses moved quickly. While oxygen was manually being pumped through the endotracheal tube by one nurse, another was checking to see if the leads to the monitor were properly attached to the body or chest. Another immediately attached a defibrillator for cardiopulmonary resuscitation (CPR). This was a medical device, battery-powered with adhesive pads. The pads were then applied to the chest to allow an electrical current to pass through the heart to reset the heart's normal current. In the OR, one was always available and ready to use.

An epinephrine, or adrenaline, shot was immediately administered by the surgeon in the hopes of reversing the cardiac arrest. They all quickly shot a glance at the monitors. Nothing was moving. The noise was a solid sound and no beeping occurred at all.

The doctor began pumping at Teresa's chest hoping that the massaging effect would kick start the heart to begin beating once again. They prepared for a second shot with the defibrillator. The doctor announced, "CLEAR," and electricity soared into Teresa's chest.

Nothing! No heartbeat! The monitor showed no signs of movement up and down. There were no beeping sounds, just that long rhythmic noise affiliated with the heart having flatlined.

Everyone continued working on Teresa no matter what was determined as final. The fifth rib resection was completed while Teresa was technically considered dead due to the time factor involved. Next was working to complete the left upper lobe lobectomy. The oxygen kept being pumped. The anesthesiologist continued monitoring even though he believed Teresa to have expired. It was now over two hours and counting. They kept working on her.

CHAPTER 11

Teresa was able to see herself lifting up. This was not her body lifting up as she saw her body on the operating table. She stared at the doctors and nurses working on her to bring her back to life. She heard the doctor say "CLEAR" and the defibrillator shooting into her body as it jerked her body up and down. But how could that happen? What was going on? Why could she see and yet not totally comprehend?

This was her soul lifting up—that tiny aura, or spark, that truly identifies as one's life forever and always. As published by physician Duncan MacDougall in 1907 entitled "The 21 Grams Experiment," he hypothesized that the human soul weighed three-quarters of an ounce or 21.3 grams when the soul departed the body.

The physical body was only for a portion of time. It was finite. The body could not last forever and always. It was not meant to last for all eternity. It was meant to learn, understand, grow, and live accordingly on the earth plane in the manner that God's infinite plan was brought forth.

It was also giving the soul the right to "free will." This encompassed innumerable choices that enabled the human being to decide, after living for a determinate time with the parents, to move forward hopefully within the laws established in society. A person would meet someone, get married, have and raise children, work, become a meaningful member of the community, and eventually pass on, hopefully and probably not always in the order discussed.

It was the soul that flourished after death and forever continued to serve in the matter that the body had lived on the earth plane. Whether as a decent human being or otherwise, this determined how it would live in the afterlife or death.

While Teresa's soul was rising from her body, it was the Holy Ghost that was bringing her out. It was the Holy Ghost that was within everyone because God was within everyone. When the soul entered the fetus during pregnancy, the Holy Ghost accompanied the soul because God was in every soul. God was with us before birth and God was a part of us at death.

As Teresa's soul was further moving away from her body, a hand reached out to her and took hold of her. At first translucent, it radiated with pure energy. Hundreds of millions of sparks of light illuminated the hand. It was not only beautiful to see but also a wonderful essence of energy. Its radiant beauty was limitless.

It was Teresa's soul taking in every detail and physicality of Jesus. She was remembering and being given the feeling of all the wounds Jesus was subjected. These were the wounds Jesus experienced for Teresa since it was Teresa now coming out of the body. Eventually all would experience these wounds.

Teresa was then going over all the wrongs she may have done during her lifetime. It might have been a hurtful outburst. It could have been a wrong acted out on another. It was as if looking back on one's entire life in a single moment and waiting for the flash of the camera to appear. It would encompass everything.

According to Teresa, "everyone must go through all the frogs of one's life before getting to the prince. All of the negative attitudes and expressions, all of the down feelings and disagreements, the hate and trash, all of it must be expunged before the soul is free to pass through to Paradise. These are 'life lessons' that everyone goes through. Until a person realizes this, the soul cannot move forward."

As it was said in every Mass, "Lord, I am not worthy," we all need to remember that we ARE worthy once we give it up and accept. Teresa added, "Your soul needs to think about YOUR EVER AFTER, not someone else's." We all need to forgive and ask for forgiveness of others. Contrition was never a bad thing. It was always giving the soul a positive motion to move forward toward paradise.

A voice then spoke out. "Come with me, my daughter."

Teresa responded automatically as if she recognized the voice. It was calm, authoritative, gentle, and supreme. She heard herself respond with just one word at first calling out to the voice, "Dad."

"I want to show you something," the voice exclaimed.

Teresa hesitated. "I need to go back into the body to fight," Teresa said. "I'm not done with the fight. There's more I need to do."

"It's going to be okay," the voice reassured her as Teresa's soul then realized it was Jesus speaking to her.

Taking in the full physicality of Jesus was beyond incredible. Every centimeter, every inch, every detail escaped her ability to describe the perfection that was given to Him through the Father. The image of the Lord had been revealed to her, but she knew the words could not be expressed with justice.

And yet Teresa's soul was reassured.

"Don't worry," He stated as she would soon comprehend a wonder to behold.

Jesus took her soul and they were gone. They just disappeared in a split second. With no thought process to examine what was being done, they vanished from the area they were.

So what is the feeling of "pure love"? It illuminates with a joy and ecstatic excitement throughout every morsel of one's soul. It is never-ending as it sparkles within every inch of the afterlife. It is all encompassing and is something not felt while living in the body even if there was total love, peace, happiness, and joy while on the earth plane. Nothing like this is ever experienced.

Think of a super nova exploding into millions upon millions, billions upon billions, of light and flashing the entire spectrum of the rainbow. Think of all the Fourth of July fireworks or New Year's fireworks celebrations. Think of every time you thought the power of your love for another would explode within your body and all you wanted was for that feeling to last forever and always.

This is even more powerful and magnificent. Spectacular isn't even a word within the realm of description. One might even say that there are no words to describe the feeling, the expression, the majesty or joy. It is much more and beyond that.

It is Divine Love. All pain, anxiety, and stress are eliminated. There is no anger, no negativity. Every pore is saturated with blissful love. It is beyond the comprehension one could feel during life. It is the epitome of what one would believe is heaven on earth, but much more magnanimous. There are only two true words to explain this feeling—just PURE LOVE.

Love that saturates through all time as time is infinite, forever and always. It is love that embraces, love that new parents "might" feel after the birth of a child, love that one feels on the day of a marriage, love that tingles, shivers, and creates a warmth felt throughout the body and MORE, so much more.

Then all of a sudden, they reappeared and were in heaven as the body of Jesus was next to her. He was the most incredible and stunning image of a man she had ever seen. Jesus was beautiful and handsome. He was flawless. He was PERFECT!

The yellow aura surrounding his head was bright sunlight. As if picturing the image in the Divine Mercy, it was even more perfect than that. Staring was not an option. One could only look and see the glorious and knowing that God was also a part since Jesus was the Son of God.

Going to heaven was as if one were going through a veil that was easily penetrated. It was as quick and simple with never a thought to how it would be done or if it could be done. There was nothing impossible to accomplish in the afterlife and heaven. It wasn't even a thought process as it was as automatic as the blinking of the eyes.

What wonder! What a phenomenal experience to behold. Jesus took the hand of the soul of Teresa-Rose Retzlaff and brought her to the most incredible place in existence in the universe. It was a place that was infinite in seemingly stupendous splendor.

There was a brightness that exuded the rays of the sun. There was the warmness with every morsel felt by her soul as only love poured out from all around. It radiated to the nth degree. It was Jesus not having to prove, but to show his daughter that heaven was as glorious and everlasting as one would even imagine.

Because "one day is like a thousand years and a thousand years is like one day," no one could or would ever want to leave this place.

It was perfect. It was even beyond perfect if one could describe what beyond perfect would even mean.

Jesus showed Teresa her mother and father. They looked as if they were when they were ten. Her father was in a backyard as a boy in knickers. He was playful. He was smiling and looked like he did not have a care in the world. Why would he? He was in heaven and in his chosen body.

She saw her family members, aunts, uncles, and grandparents. Everyone was as they wanted to be and knew they were a family. There was happiness and contentment. There was only love pouring out from them all. It was the closeness and devotion of what a family should be on earth.

Teresa couldn't understand fully the authenticity of such a place. Jesus showed her what life after death could be and would be. It was a place of harmony where everyone was happy, serene, and a part of the heavenly miracle of God, Jesus Christ, and the Holy Ghost. It was so much more than what was being described by a person of authority, mainly a priest, yearning for the understanding to live as blessed as possible.

If only everyone could comprehend that life on earth could be a place of total love and peace. If only egos could be erased to accept everyone as they were, no hatred of those of a different color, creed, or sex, and no determination of one race to dominate another. That true meaning of the second commandment to "love thy neighbor as thyself"—this was what Jesus was revealing to Teresa at this very moment. This was the supreme, ultimate knowledge of wisdom that was always explained when reading the Bible.

Imagine what Solomon asked God in 2 Chronicles 1:11–12 (NKJV): "And God said to Solomon: 'Because this was in your heart, and you have not asked for riches or wealth or honour or the life of your enemies, nor have you asked for long life; but have asked wisdom and knowledge for yourself, that you may judge my people over whom I have made you king (12).'"

CHAPTER 12

Jesus then spoke out and said, "I need you to see other things."

What other things? Teresa thought. *What could be better than this? A family together without a care in the world and all loving.*

There was not a tear among them. Teresa knew she wanted this. She could tell Jesus to just drop her off here and move on to the next soul. This life-after-death experience was all she needed forever and always.

Going back to the discords with her husband, the continued traumas and stress of her disease, and the worries she has put on her family, sisters and brothers, would be a thing of the past. Living in heaven would truly be "heaven-sent" and now realized. Teresa did not want to wait any longer.

She could wait for the rest of her family when it was their time. She would greet them all when they arrived. She would greet everyone and anyone. She could be known as the "Master Greeter" if Jesus Christ would let her. They would be as amazed at the miraculous and glorious as she was. She would be their ambassador to the everlasting. Her sisters and brothers would be distraught at having lost their sister on the earth plane. Her children would be devastated at having no mother to comfort and protect them. In reality, who knew what Tim would think or believe or even do without a wife? Teresa didn't want to think about these things any longer. She felt she didn't need to.

But Holy, Heavenly Blessed Jesus Christ! This was a moment that Teresa wanted now and evermore. She didn't need to go back into her body. All the pain, anxiety, stress, and heartaches were gone. Love was all she felt. And love was all she needed. Then Jesus took her hand, and the images faded as quickly as the veil going to heaven.

Again, with just the blink of the eye, the mood changed. The golden images turned to darkness. It was hot. Very hot. Uncomfortably hot. Not hot as hell, but Teresa knew this was purgatory.

Teresa saw the flames rising in all places. It was like being in an incinerator with souls wrapped in the heat coming and going in agony. They writhed in pain waiting for their chance and yearning for their time to go to heaven.

How long, oh, Lord? they thought. *When will I earn that reward? Give me another chance and I will repent, as Ebeneezer Scrooge did, and prove to you that I can change. I'll share everything with Lazarus and all the poor.*

One could analogize it when Shadrach, Meshach, and Abednego being thrown into the fiery pit during the time as told in the Book of Daniel in the Old Testament.

> They refused to bow down to the golden idol that King Nebuchadnezzar had made. He ordered his men to make the furnace seven times hotter than normal…
>
> Even some of the guards were killed during the preparations to make the furnace seven times hotter. Shadrach, Meshach and Abednego were to burn within minutes as the King went to see the ashes of the men…
>
> However, when King Nebuchadnezzar looked into the furnace, he saw not three, but four walking around and unharmed. It was later believed that an angel was with the three and protected them. The king then realized the power of God Almighty, the One worshipped by Shadrach, Meshach and Abednego.

Teresa stared as the souls wrapped in the fiery furnace waited without knowing when their time would come to enter the kingdom of heaven. In purgatory, all can eventually reach that time when their souls have been forgiven and repented and earned the right to be freed from purgatory. Their time on earth was not one of continuous atrocities inflicted on others.

Purgatory was for those souls of the men and women who committed crimes not unforgivable or unrepentable. Souls who pray for forgiveness and understand that they have the power to move into heaven must comprehend that God Almighty and Jesus Christ want all souls into heaven. They must believe and rise up to be better.

It was for other souls that Jesus wanted to show Teresa next. Jesus said, "I want to show you something you will not be happy." Although Teresa did not respond, she was probably thinking that she did not want to see anymore. She wanted Jesus to reverse course and go back through the veil and to heaven. *Just let me be with the light*, she thought. *Let me rejoice in knowing and praying to God Almighty and His Son always and forever.*

Jesus continued and Teresa followed without words. It was not like she could object anyway since He was in charge and the entire reasons were not yet revealed to her. There would be more to see whether she enjoyed it or not.

He showed her earth. He showed her murders and other crimes. All levels of what would be considered such evil being poured out from one human being to another. List any of the crimes that cause others to be inflicted by deranged and damaged individuals and that was the first level of hell.

First level of hell? You mean there was more? Teresa thought.

Jesus also showed Teresa the next level. That was what was considered "below earth." These existed in the forms of other atrocities even more heinous than the first level. The list was endless. It included molestation, pedophilia, castration, extermination, sexual slavery, endless rape, and torture. There were so many more putrid and horrendous acts that most people would not even recognize they even existed. The worst of evil, where the crimes went on for minutes, hours, and even days that were inflicted on poor unsuspecting human beings came into view. How sad that these deviants couldn't even think of what would happen to them after they died.

Read *Helter Skelter*, the Jeffrey Dahmer atrocities, the time of Hitler and Putin and all who followed in their warped and evil minds with no thought or iota of remorse. Those who felt they had escaped the wrath of the evil after the war or after their reign of torture would never know the love and joy of heaven after death. How many actually thought like this? How many disgusting, morbid, and unforgiving human beings fled to South America after World War II? How many deaths were inflicted on those by Saddam Hussein who wanted to control all of Iraq without consequences? What about the lives destroyed in the 9/11 attacks? Did those who devised and carry out their plans even think there would not be consequences?

They may think they escaped the evils of their past. Their wanting to forget and live without consequences would not last forever. They would pass on from the earth plane. They would meet their "Maker." They would end up in hell whether they felt otherwise. Their souls had to know that the result would be nothing close to heaven.

Remember, Teresa explained that the Holy Ghost is with everyone in the beginning of life because God is inside everyone. What a person decides to do with their life is free will. It is a conscious decision to do good or do evil. It is also a conscious decision to be contrite, ask for forgiveness, and repent.

Those were only examples of modern-day tragedies. They were worse than tragedies. They were holocausts in their own right. However, there were numerous atrocities throughout all of history. Too numerous to mention, they all represented individuals who never understood or even thought about "eternal life."

They had no thoughts of life after death. Living with the ill-gotten gains from their crimes and fleeing to another country would not be the end of it all. They would experience only HELL no matter how far they felt they escaped the atrocities of that which they controlled in the past or even in today's atrocities of Ukraine, Israel, Palestine, and so many other places where evil flourished.

As explained to me by Teresa, "A forgiven mortal sin goes to purgatory. Not a forgiven mortal sin? Hell! The reason there is confession is really to give us back the grace we lose when we commit mortal and venial sins. When you attend Mass, venial sins are forgiven with the Confiteor, or Confession of Faith, when the priest forgives every one of their venial sins. If you go to a Latin Mass, your sins are forgiven twice in the Mass, once at the beginning and once right before communion for bad thoughts or others, during the Mass."

Terrified and horrified, Teresa pleaded with Jesus to stop. She wanted to go back to heaven where everything was beautiful, peaceful, and "heavenly" in the sense that God and Jesus Christ were in charge of the most wonderful "forever after." Being a part of the eternal brightness and living in grace were beyond comparison to what Jesus what showing her at this moment.

"I just want you to understand and believe," Jesus explained, "the divine love that I feel for you. You understanding the difference between pure love and pure evil is important."

Teresa did understand the "total" meaning of the words while alive on earth. Now after seeing and experiencing all that Jesus was showing her, Teresa knew that her life was not evil, but good. It was nowhere near pure evil. She was a good person. She was a good mother. Her decisions in her life of becoming an OR nurse anesthetist and helping others to heal and raising a family were the correct choices. Even her choice of being unfaithful was not an unforgiveable sin. Tim's choices of being cruel and abusive were not unforgiveable sins. However, he had or needed to acknowledge them and confess these sins. Both needed to repent and ask for forgiveness.

"Come with me," Jesus said and took Teresa away from the images of hell.

Then Jesus explained, "Like a father takes a child's hand, this I ask of you as a loving father. I want you to pray for me. Pray for others. This is your mission. It is something I need you to do. You will see miracles."

Teresa said nothing but only continued to listen. In the back of her soul, if there was a "back," as she was listening to the words, she did wonder what miracles she would see. Being with Jesus was already a miracle. Experiencing, firsthand so to speak, the true beauty of the Lord Jesus Christ and wanting to only pray for Him, as he said, would be giving the glory and honor Jesus deserved. She would, naturally, also pray for others. She had done this continually while alive on earth.

"You are the first miracle," Jesus told her.

What? Teresa thought. It was then that Teresa totally understood Jesus's meaning in the words He spoke. *Wait!* she thought. *Haven't I been gone too long? What…*

Before being able to utter another word, Teresa was sent back into her body. It was the Holy Ghost that brought her back to life by breathing into the body using her own breath. Her soul knew what to do. It would follow the directions of the Lord.

Jesus said, "It was her mission and she would be the first miracle. You will see many miracles."

The monitors immediately reacted informing the doctors and nurses that the patient was alive. However, Teresa was now covered with a sheet as they had declared her dead. It was now over three hours and twenty minutes since her heart had stopped pumping life into her body. The fifth rib resection and the upper lobe lobectomy were completed long ago.

While it felt like a millisecond and an eternity all at the same time, Teresa was alive and breathing on her own. The miracle of knowing and conversing with the Lord Jesus Christ was the ultimate experience she could ever know while back on earth. There would be so much to do. There were unsaid promises to keep.

There would be people looking at her as if she were crazy and wanting to be as far away from her as possible. Then there would be people who would want to be as close to her and hear the words of Jesus Christ. Teresa would open her mouth, smile, and bring in as many as would be possible. The glory of the Lord Jesus Christ would be spoken by a wonderful, chosen soul.

There would be those who would not believe and provide reasonable excuses for her "medical" miracle. There would be those praising God and the Lord Jesus Christ for giving Teresa back to her family and celebrating life. Many would pray and rejoice in knowing that God and the Lord Jesus Christ were alive and this could be the catalyst for reforming a doubtful mind.

But when Teresa opened her eyes and felt the sheet covering her body, she inhaled a huge breath and said just three words after the endotracheal tube was removed, "GOD IS GREAT!"

CHAPTER 13

The medical staff working on Teresa for those three hours and twenty minutes were in total disbelief.

"Did you hear that?" a female intern asked.

There was now the thoracic surgeon and male assistant, two male residents, one female intern, the anesthesiologist, and a pulmonologist. All the monitors were flashing numbers, and the ECG was showing a heartbeat. All wondered if they heard the words that supposedly echoed throughout the OR. They stared at the medical instruments and wanted to verify what they were seeing by inching closer.

For what? A better look?

Did the words come out from the patient that was covered with a sheet over her body and supposedly dead? Questioning if they had heard without error and double-checking all the instruments to see what they may have missed, apprehension was coming across their minds as the room stood silent.

Was this real? The dead was now talking back? Were they living in a dream? Or nightmare? Someone looked at the clock and again noted the time. It was more than three hours and thirty minutes now.

Slowly removing the sheet over Teresa's head and staring at the patient now awake on the operating table, only the main doctor said two words in response, "Praise God."

They were tired. They were more than tired. They were exhausted. After going through and experiencing in awe according to the lead doctor, a great sigh of relief was now felt in the OR. They could feel their own blood pressures coming down. The level of stress going through their veins subsided. As if they all were holding their breaths, the coolness of the OR took over, and the inner heat leveled off within their own bodies. Who knew how many stories would be told after removing the patient from the OR and into the recovery room? Each member of the medical team might have their own opinion, medically or otherwise, as to the results and observations once they cleaned up, took off the surgical garments, and even exited the hospital once relieved of their shifts.

It was as if they all would get in their cars, drive home or to a bar, and greet their respective spouses or significant others, children, and friends, and the first words out of their mouths would be, "You'll never even guess how my day went or what occurred."

Before any questions would be asked or responses would be received, each would spew out or stutter, "I witnessed a miracle today. I kid you not, it was a miracle… I need a drink."

First Teresa did need to be cleaned up and taken into the recovery room. They needed to make sure she was comfortable and without pain. Her vitals were to be monitored every fifteen minutes just in case.

In case of what? In case she has a heart attack? In case her vitals fall back into emergency status? How about all of the above?

For Teresa, she was going over the entire episode, anomaly and spiritual awakening, that she had just experienced. She remembered her soul saying she did not want to go back. Her mind recalled every word Jesus had said, verbatim and without hesitation. It was crystal clear in her mind what she was to accomplish as the words "you are the first miracle" echoed flawlessly.

After being showed all the levels, Teresa knew that purgatory, the earth, and below earth were not options for her. She also knew that had there been any iota of doubt that a tiny spec of what she believed in the past were hopeful wishes, all those thoughts were now put out in the pasture. While she never personally doubted, Teresa knew Jesus was real.

Even though everyone, at some point, questions or confronts the frailties of their faith, most are assured through belief in prayer and their educational and spiritual practices that God Almighty and the Lord Jesus Christ are not just figments to be referenced. They are physical, mental, and practical means for a harmonious and structured life. All the laws, all the commandments, all the educational texts, and learning facilities are provided for a lifetime. The ultimate goal is not only heaven on earth but also heaven after death.

Teresa would do all that Jesus told her. Following the instructions of the Lord Jesus Christ was paramount to everyday living. Whether those she spoke with believed or did not believe, she would pray "ceaselessly" as it was said in the Bible. Even if she could not convince the "doubting Thomas's," Teresa would have the medical documents to prove her case. She was the first miracle and knew the truth whether or not they believed.

Her soul had seen her siblings on the patio outside of the waiting room and also those still in the waiting room needing to hear of the outcome of the operation, good or otherwise. Her sister Jacquie kept saying, "Something is not right. This is taking too long. I don't like what I am feeling."

Teresa was wheeled into "isolation recovery" after surgery. There was a large glass window and door. Due to the trauma of the miracle, she needed to be monitored and watched for some time as there may be issues with the patient after she was fully cognizant and aware of what occurred. The medical team required to watch Teresa needed to be prepared. Just in case a bell or whistle went off, split-second and immediate reactions needed to kick in.

When the doctor finally came out of the OR and confronted the family, it was only news of success. The operations were successful, and Teresa was now in the isolation recovery area. They could see her in a short while once she was brought to her own room in the hospital.

The doctor added that it became a bit difficult for a while but that she would recover and the coccidioidomycosis was cleared. Nothing else was said since all that was needed was to hear that their daughter, wife, and sister was doing well. He figured that it would be Teresa who would tell of the experience.

The Holy Ghost said, "There is something you must do." The instructions were embedded into her mind. It was "Pray for intentions. Talk to people about their lives without getting personal. But you must pray. Pray for your family, your neighbor's family, your parish's family. Pray for the homeless, the hungry, the homebound, the infirm. Most people wonder if their prayers are being answered. Assure them that their prayers are being heard and answered. While it may not be in their time, it is in God's time."

She saw a notebook filled with people she must pray for. It included anybody and everybody. She would add to the book the new names daily. This included those she would meet, those needing new intentions, and those looking for a gentle voice to listen to. Again, it was anybody and everybody.

Speaking to one of the priests at Holy Trinity Catholic Church in Northern Virginia, Father Carr had terrible allergies. Teresa began praying for the allergies to be removed. The next time she spoke with Father Carr, he confirmed the allergies were cleared. This was just one of the "miracles" she supposed she was to see. So much more had been revealed and asked of her during the meeting with the Holy Ghost before awakening. She was to attend the Novus Ordo or New Mass. The Protestanization of the Catholic Church was ongoing. There were many prayers that were removed due to Vatican II and Pope Francis. She was to go to Latin Mass where all the prayers were still part of the Mass.

Instead of focusing on heaven, Teresa was to focus on "human will" and not "divine will." It was human will that was empowered after Vatican II. Humans wanted more power, and the church was giving it to them. They felt this would bring more people back to Mass. They could follow and voice along within the Mass.

However, this was not in the original doctrine prior to Vatican II. It should have always remained with divine will. The will of God Almighty and Lord Jesus Christ should not be misinterpreted so as to give humans the glory. What glory could there possibly be in providing such miraculous tenets to humans?

If the church wanted more patronage to Mass, the teachings of the Lord Jesus Christ, the writings from the New Testament, which included the gospels of the apostles, should be explained to appeal to the masses in a more contemporary fashion. Maybe they didn't fully understand. Maybe the modern interpretations were not fully clarified.

Possibly they were over clarified, or simplified, to the point where it was becoming too elementary and boring. Just possibly, many questions had not been answered. There were numerous excuses why people no longer felt comfortable. In any of the circumstances, modern-day human life was relying more on electronic, social media, and various other reasons for the decrease of patronage to the church. Something needed to change. Teresa needed to be a part of that change.

Teresa's mind was filled with the Spirit of Jesus Christ, God Almighty, and the Holy Ghost. It was in the recovery room that so much was remembered. It was also a new beginning for her. It was the design of Jesus to bring this miracle to the masses and reveal all that was not only needed but also required to live according to HIS words.

Teresa knew where to begin, again, now that she was brought back to life. First she needed to heal, recover, and get out of the hospital. There was one major obstacle holding her back after they brought her to the isolation room. She was nonverbal.

RICHARD PARNES

Teresa in 1984

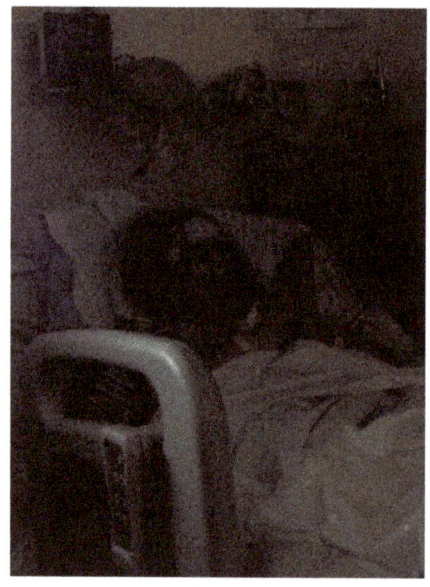

Teresa after 1st surgery

MY LAZARUS LIFE

Teresa at 34

Teresa in 2021

Autumn, Timmy ll and Joey

Teresa's Sibling; Top l to r. Ricky, Mary and Michael; next row, Jacquie Jr., Jonni-Ann, Teresa-Rose

Daniel Earp

Teresa and John at a banquet

RICHARD PARNES

picture taken by Christopher Robin, photographer

Golden picture of Jesus

MY LAZARUS LIFE

Teresa's mother Jacqueline

Greg, Teresa and Richard at Gainsville Diner

CHAPTER 14

As previously stated, while in the isolation room, Teresa needed to be monitored 24/7. Even the doctors didn't know how long she would be there. In the first place, they needed to hear her speak. No words came out of her mouth the entire time she had spent in isolation. At first it was very precarious. Too many questions formulated in the minds of the medical staff—questions they couldn't answer but would only surmise.

"Anyone heard anything?" one nurse would ask.

"Not yet," another would answer. "Any movement from the patient?"

"Movement? Yes! Speech? No!"

"Should we test for brain malfunctions at this time?"

"Not yet. Still too soon. Pulse and BP are normal. Just wish we would hear something."

This was the conversation for quite some time. Any medical personnel who entered Teresa's room for the purpose of observing needed to write down anything and everything. If there was nothing to write, write it down. Her surgeon also needed to allow for her lung to heal. It was thought that possibly she was nonverbal because speech was too painful with the lung not having fully healed. Maybe taking in air was too painful, so she decided not to speak.

Eventually, she was transferred to ICU. Teresa spent two to three weeks in ICU, and still no words came out of her mouth. All tests showed that the lung had healed and was fully functional. The doctors and nurses watched for movements or signs that would show improvement.

Day after day, they questioned one another. Thoughts roamed through their heads that maybe there might have been brain damage. However, no trauma showed on Teresa's face. In fact, she looked tranquil and "heavenly"—heavenly in a sense that she was one with God, Jesus, and herself. No one could even imagine that she was in constant contact with the Lord Jesus Christ and having wonderful conversations.

After being brought into ICU, her family was able to see her. While the visits couldn't last too long, her brothers and sisters wanted to be there. They wanted to make sure she was doing well. Being with her would surely be a good sign, and maybe Teresa would finally speak.

Teresa would listen each day to family discussions. She could learn how her children were doing and knowing that they were safe. With everything on the positive side, Teresa just had an elegant air of tranquility on her face. She was feeling pensive and even spiritual. She was fully relaxed. Life was going well in her mind. And why wouldn't it be going well? She had just spent an indeterminate amount of time with the Lord Jesus Christ. The Holy Ghost had breathed life back into her. There were numerous angels all around protecting her. She looked great, serene, and at peace!

So why do I need to speak? was all she thought. *I've just seen God! Jesus speaks to me all the time. What more could I possibly want at this time?*

If it had been up to her, she wouldn't want for anything except being with Jesus and her angels day in and day out. Her reality was that they were with her every day, every night, in her dreams, and a part of everything she did.

Teresa was then sent to a psyche ward. It had come to the point where other professionals would need to evaluate her. Something was just not coming together, and it had come to the point where it was out of the hands of the OR, isolation, and ICU medical staff. It was time for psychiatrists and psychologists. Without speech, Teresa could not be released to go home.

In the psyche ward, Teresa could hear her angels, and in fact God, still talking with her. Wonderful conversations would take place. The facial movements surrounding her lips were serene. There were smiles, grins, light laughter under her breath, and a full twinkle of her eyes. Teresa was enjoying the miracles daily.

After six months, she began blurting out and talking nonsense. Nothing seemed to make sense as she was, in her mind, just toying with wanting to inform people what she had gone through. Teresa did mention that there was one person who did understand the "blurting out" and "nonsensical talking." That was her mother.

Her mother was of that "devout nature." Ecumenical since moving to Barstow, her mother still considered herself Catholic. But she still went to many churches. "God reaches out to everyone," she would say as she would bring her music and play the organ.

None of the members of the other churches even realized they were being converted to Catholicism through music.

Her mother knew it was in God's time that Teresa would be fully healed, and the sound of her voice would be heard. There was no rush. She was safe. She was protected by her angels. She was conversing daily with Jesus. He would tell her when.

Teresa understood and knew everything that was happening to those her mother touched. She was doing the work he had chosen for her. God Almighty and the Lord Jesus Christ moved in many different ways. One religion did not own them. The Bible was spoken in all churches. Music was sung in all churches. It might not be the way of the Catholic Church. However, bringing others together to praise the Lord Jesus Christ, God Almighty, and reach for the Holy Ghost could also be felt in all churches. This was whether they believe in the Holy Trinity or not. And wasn't this the proclamation of Jesus Christ when He announced the second commandment and spoke to "love thy neighbor as thyself"?

Even the Beatles sang it beautifully when they performed "Love Is All You Need." Although the middle 1950s, 1960s, and 1970s were turbulent times with the Vietnam War, the main theme within the music industry was a constant mood and call for peace, harmony, spirituality, and love.

Peace and love were the main themes during Woodstock Music and Art Fair in Bethel, New York, forty miles from the town of Woodstock. The crowds were immense as 500,000 screaming and loving fans gathered. Although it was deemed a huge success as the counterculture movement of the 1960s, bad weather, sex, and drugs caused huge headaches for the authorities. Even today, the peaceful celebration was still renowned in history.

So to "love thy neighbor as thyself" meant that all faiths needed to come together and bring peace to all believers in the world. Teresa needed to get well and bring together all to know God and the Lord Jesus Christ. Even in the psyche ward, she heard these words regularly.

Teresa was in the psyche ward for six months. Her brother Mike would say, "She's having good days. She's seeing God."

Her sister Mary said, "Maybe she is seeing God."

After a certain amount of time, all the speculation stopped. They didn't want people to think that Teresa was insane. In Teresa's mind, she just smiled and listened to the conversations she was having with Jesus. She was not insane and would eventually prove it. For now, the melancholy air in her mind outweighed the medicinal realities in the hospital.

Later, Teresa was sent to a physical rehab center to begin learning how to walk again. Her lung was fully healed and working as all lungs should. Learning to walk should be, excuse the pun, a "walk in the park."

This didn't take long. Teresa was back with her family and now in Needles. Although this was not what her family wanted, her children were safe. They were with their mother. They could feel the love and security she expressed to them each day. She was fully recuperated.

The disease of coccidioidomycosis was long gone. Teresa's nightmare was over.

CHAPTER 15

As for Tim, having his wife back at home was another issue. Their marriage had been on the rocks even before the surgery. One would like to believe that being apart would make the heart grow fonder—not with Tim.

He abruptly announced that the family would be moving to Hesperia, and he would begin his new position with the San Bernardino County Sheriff's Department. His training has been completed. His assignment was inside the Glen Helen Rehabilitation Center. There was just the observing and care for the inmates who were going through the process of being able to return to society and hopefully make something of themselves.

Was this actually something better for Tim and his family? Not only was he not playing the devoted husband, but also he was screwing up in every way possible. He wasn't being the father that the children needed. They needed a babysitter to watch Joey. Then Autumn and Tim II went to school and did their own "things." But Tim? He was difficult. He was uncomfortable to be around. He thought only of himself.

If there was good news to ever be associated with their marriage, it was that Teresa was back to work, Tim was working, and the idea that life was normal lasted for about eight months. Everyday issues concerning the children, family, and friends went, technically, without a hitch. There were the normal familial arguments and disagreements. When a babysitter was needed, it was a family member or an individual that Tim had found through work.

After, while in Hesperia, California, Teresa also began having a new problem. It wasn't the return of coccidioidomycosis, but it still involved the lungs. She was actually in the process of divorcing

Tim and moving back to Barstow with her family where her mother wanted her and the children.

During that time, air had improperly entered the space between the chest wall and lungs. This was called pneumothorax. It was dangerous and could be lethal. It could occur if there was excess pressure on the lungs or if a lung disease such as chronic obstructive pulmonary disease (COPD) was involved.

Teresa found herself, again, in the hospital. However, it was now in San Bernardino County Hospital where she had worked as a nurse. It was also where the medical staff still knew her and remembered her. It was where Teresa suffered a second flatline.

As usual, Teresa was prepped and ready. All questions were given answers. There were no doubts that the medical staff was prepared and Teresa was ready to finally do whatever was required to bring her to a full healthy body and be rid of any lung diseases. No one was prepared for Teresa to flatline again.

But flatline she did.

The lead surgeon worked fast to bring Teresa back to life. The nurses did what they could to get the heart pumping again. After fifteen minutes, Teresa was pronounced dead…again!

The operating room went silent. No one could believe that with such a routine surgery, Teresa would flatline and the medical staff wouldn't be able to bring her back. Nothing went wrong with the procedure. It was considered rote in all of their minds. So what went wrong?

The second time, Teresa's soul could actually feel the physicality of the hand of Jesus lifting her up. That's how she knew and understood that Jesus and Mother Mary were both with her. Teresa's soul felt as if both were taking her up to heaven. She thought this could finally be it. She would be free of disease and living in the afterlife forevermore. What a wonderful feeling and thought.

Teresa was able to see more of the glory of heaven. All the colors of the rainbow were distinct and pure. All negativity was erased and pure love received like it only existed for her as she felt cleansed of all the ills that surrounded her on earth. Moving along with ease and wonder, she was again shown all the evil in the world. Again, she was also able to stare at the beauty that surrounded the world. Teresa could feel the spirituality throughout the people as she watched before and after they entered a confessional. While penance was being completed, she could see the dust being eliminated and the grace returning to the person.

Had anyone ever seen this before? Was anyone ever given the glory to view such wonder that existed during a person's trials and tribulation? That's what it seemed! That was the true inspiration with knowing God Almighty and the Lord Jesus Christ.

As if her soul was smiling and eternal gladness would last forever, Teresa felt it. It was miniscule but profound. It was happening again and she couldn't object or ask for a reversal of decision. The Holy Ghost took her back.

Immediately, there was a change in the attitude of the lead surgeon. He heard a voice, as loud as could possibly be, telling him not to give up.

"You will bring her back to life," the voice ordered. Listening to the voice as he had never thought or believed he ever would, the doctor took a knife and cut an opening in Teresa's chest, on the left and under the breast. He would be performing a thoracotomy. This was a surgical procedure to gain access into the pleural space of the chest.

One nurse blurted out after seeing the knife in the doctor's hand and the opening in the chest, "What are you doing?"

Without responding to the nurse, the doctor then grabbed a tube and began shoving it into Teresa's chest and toward the left lung. He pushed a little farther, and the left lung expanded. He worked on Teresa for about an hour as the voice told him again, **"Do not give up."**

The only thing the doctor said under his breath was, *No!* What he thought was, *Why would I give up? I'm almost done and I'm listening to this inner voice. Giving up is not an option.*

It was then that Teresa began breathing again. The monitors were now beeping as if the patient had never flatlined. Teresa was alive…once again.

When asked by the nurse after the surgery what he heard, the doctor just shook his head.

"I was told not to give up." He then paused and thought for only a moment. "And I'm an atheist."

Teresa was brought out of surgery and rolled into a hospital room where she stayed for a week. Afterward, it was back in Hesperia with her children and…Tim.

CHAPTER 16

Now that Teresa was safe and no longer in danger, she began to sum up her medical misfortunes and blessings—misfortunes because her health had been questionable for quite some time. The conclusions were easily reached in that the coccidioidomycosis was gone. Her lungs cleared, and she was breathing normally. The pneumothorax issues were gone. The air that had entered between her chest and her lungs was cleared, her left lung inflated, and she was breathing normally again. *Anything else*, she thought. *Nope!* Teresa moved on to the blessings. The answers to these were more than easily reached. Teresa was receiving messages and speaking to Jesus Christ every day. Her angels were watching over her 24/7, and her life was getting back on track, spiritually, that is. Her children were doing well since they were so pleased that their mom was with them, finally, without other medical issues. Teresa could go back to work in a short time after a few weeks of rest and relaxation. She could proceed with life knowing that her spiritual angels kept her in the right direction as long as she listened and followed according to the instructions provided by the Lord Jesus Christ.

The final issue was Tim.

Although he seemed to be doing well at Glen Helen Rehabilitation Center in Devore, Teresa just didn't seem to be getting positive signals. Whenever Teresa felt uncertainty, it was just a matter of time before, excuse the saying, "the devil would get his due."

Sure enough, a large news story came out concerning five deputies from the San Bernardino County Sheriff's Department. All five deputies were put on leave as the news broke out that it concerned sex with a minor. One of the five deputies was none other than Teresa's problematic husband, Tim.

One of the things that were allowed within the sheriff's department was to permit the ride-along of young individuals working within the Explorer Scouts. These teens, aged fourteen to eighteen, who might want to learn more about law enforcement or help with troubled teens currently in the system, could ride in a sheriff's vehicle. They could also work within other areas of the department. There was one young female teen who did such work. As it turned out, she also provided unauthorized intimate actions to five deputies. Tim, being one of them, was caught after having been with this young woman. It also was noted that she was only seventeen and was two weeks from reaching the legal age. In as much as one would have been wise to wait until the legal age of consent was reached, even then it would have been deemed inappropriate.

There was one incident when Tim II had even said to his mom that the girl told him his father was in love with her. This was while Tim II was playing in the backyard. She walked outside and proudly announced to him about their relationship. Almost immediately, the news expanded throughout all of Los Angeles, which was in a different county, and throughout all of Southern California. The very next day, it blew up to include the entire country. It was almost a nonstop news report that could be seen on any of the local news channels as well as the cable news networks.

The authorities were pouncing on the report and demanding a full investigation. Some reported that there would be firings at the top of the sheriff's department. This was obviously not something that was going to go away with a Santa Ana wind should one have been forecast by the weather reports. When Teresa had found out about this, it was almost the final straw that broke the camel's back. Tim was arrested along with the other four deputies as the authorities went to all five homes. The worst part was that Teresa's children were with Tim at the time.

Teresa was working. She was out of the house and was angry as any mother and wife could be after learning of the story. Adding insult to injury, Teresa's children were taken into a foster home.

Her only words to Tim, when she finally confronted him, were stern and direct. "If you plead no contest or guilty, I'll leave you."

Four of the five deputies were able to save their jobs with a plea that provided a suspension for six months and no contact with anyone under the age of eighteen. One could immediately guess who the fifth deputy was. Despite the warning given to him, Tim, as stubborn and maybe as stupid as could be, pleaded no contest.

No contest? Teresa thought. *Did my husband not hear what I said? Did he not see how the others saved their jobs and were able to move on after their suspension? What in God's name is going on in his head?* Teresa's thoughts moved a mile a minute. She couldn't believe the ignorance, or stupidity, of her husband.

Be that as it may, Teresa eventually moved back to Barstow with her children. When it was determined that the babysitter voiced to Teresa that she was in love with Tim, Teresa had only four words for her—"You can have him."

Teresa filed for divorce, had the marriage annulled, and was officially rid of Tim Retzlaff. Now she had to move on. Hopefully, there would be no more surprises medically or "otherwise"—otherwise being the wrong man in her life.

CHAPTER 17

Now that they were back in Barstow, again, and settled in, Teresa was still working where her reputation and her services were greatly needed. Her employers were very pleased to know that she could continue the excellent work she always gave. Tim being out of her life was a blessing.

Once more, with all the traveling Teresa had to do with her nursing jobs, it soon became a redundant thought that moving again may be in their immediate future. This was not a problem for Teresa as her life was accustomed to frequent relocations.

Autumn, on the other hand, hated the idea of moving again. She voiced her objections as her schooling, her friends, and her entire life was consistently being upended. She wanted to be a normal teenager.

There were constant discussions between Jesus and Teresa once she was out of the hospital. She was reminded every day to listen to the instructions that had been provided. She was told to speak and pray for everyone. She needed to talk with many.

She needed to write down their intentions. She needed to follow through without the slight objection that may pop up in her mind since there were many individuals and souls needing to know that Jesus Christ loved them.

Her sisters, brothers, and mother were there to make sure the love and care would never leave. Even though her siblings had their own families, the entire unit was a team. How wonderful it felt that being brought up with caring parents who espoused God and family would stay forever and always to all who truly mattered. Those conversations with family commenced with the usual closeness that they had throughout their lives.

They had moved from one side of the country to the other as a family sans the father. They had again moved three more times, with the father and as a family. Children grew up and became adults. Colleges were attended, careers were built, and soon grandchildren were born. It was always family first. This was the way her mother always wanted it.

When Tim was gone, it was like breathing fresh air. Her family couldn't stand the way he treated her and kept wondering when the time would come to let go. At this point in their lives, they were glad that it was NOW!

Tim had developed a nickname for Teresa long ago. It was Bitch. It didn't make sense at first. He had never displayed this type of disrespect in high school. They were typical high school sweethearts. When had he decided it was okay to call her such a horrible name? This was love? Only to Tim.

Asking him to stop was only made worse when he would say it was "his way of saying that he loved her." He would continue to call her this everywhere they went. It was "kind of like a joke." Teresa had told him she didn't like it, but he wasn't listening.

The family requested he stop while in their presence. Tim made everyone feel uncomfortable and questions why she would have married such a disgusting human being would or could never be answered.

Thank the Lord Jesus Christ! Teresa had the marriage annulled after the divorce so there wouldn't be any reference to him. Autumn, Timothy II, and Joey were pleased. Timothy had changed the calling of his name from the shortened version. He also didn't mind Timmy.

He couldn't stand his father. He was never a good father. Why even reference him in any conversation? Even having him in the house as a surrogate male figure was soon out of the question. Hearing from her angels, who watched over her, Teresa's patience paid off, and she was now free to move ahead with her life.

Many spiritual things did change for Teresa once out of the hospital. The most important was that Jesus would take her out of the body and would speak with her. This was also done with the kids trying to speak with her.

"Mom!" Autumn would say. No answer.

"Mom, let's go out and get something to eat for dinner. Let's get a hamburger," Timmy would blurt out. Again no answer.

Jesus informed Teresa that angels would be watching over them. Her children could even see the angels, especially Timmy! However, Teresa wasn't able to see the angels at first.

It seemed to become some kind of game for Autumn, Timmy, and Joey. Autumn would smile and innocently play with them. Joey would just laugh a bellyful. Timmy was so engrossed at times with them. He was considered a genius as his discussions would be off in another world. They all loved their angels. They felt warm and safe whenever they were around. The good news was that they were always near and watching.

CHAPTER 18

All stories would hope for a happy ending where life would move on and normalcy would become the day. This did not happen, at this time, for Teresa. Life was moving swiftly with two jobs. The traversing I-15 south to I-10 toward her nursing job at San Bernardino County Hospital and then going back the same route to Victor Valley Community Hospital in Victorville took its toll on her.

Just as a reference, Victorville was south of Barstow about thirty to forty minutes. It would take another hour to get to I-10, south from the I-15, and to San Bernardino County Hospital. The long hours at work, along with long hours on the freeways, became overwhelming for her. She needed to shorten the driving time.

As one would guess, Teresa moved again to Victorville, California. This was a thriving, growing small city that branched not only east of the I-15 but also to the west. On both sides of the freeway, new communities were sprouting up all over the desert. Since costs were going up dramatically in the Los Angeles area, many families were moving to the desert communities for the suburban/rural feel.

The suburban/rural feel would cost these newly transitioned families almost two hours by car to get to their jobs if they worked on the west side of Los Angeles. The good news was that companies were providing vanpools to and from work. Some had to actually wake up at three in the morning to be at work by six thirty or seven.

Suburban because so much was being built and I-15 traffic was increasing. Rural was due to the time one could spend driving east or west. Go as little as five miles in either direction and one would see nothing but singlewide or doublewide trailers hooked up to electricity and water. There were also some very nice homes out in the middle of nowhere fully fenced off from the outside world.

In Teresa's case, an apartment would suffice. It did decrease the time that was spent getting to both jobs. With the coccidioidomycosis fully cured and no chance of it coming back, traveling was almost carefree. She now had air-conditioning in the car she drove. Family was once again able to help when required.

Autumn, on the other hand, refused to move again. She was doing well in school and wanted continuity as she was approaching high school. Barstow was "it." Living with her aunt was fine.

Teresa, on the other hand, was a workaholic. With a little bit of money now saved, she was able to enjoy a few things for herself. Having been a sports fan all her life, she was a fanatic when it came to the Dodgers for baseball, Kings for hockey, and Lakers for basketball. At times, she went to see all three teams.

In the 1980s, tickets were not the astronomical prices they've become. As a matter of fact, before the Los Angeles Lakers won the title in 1985 with Magic Johnson, a season single seat two levels up and center court would only cost $40 per game. The next year, it went up to $400 per game. It became crazy to pay those kinds of prices even back in 1986. Now for the most part, corporations purchase the seats and hand them out to their employees. Baseball and ice hockey also became ridiculous when discussing prices. During the time of Mike Scioscia as the catcher and Steve Garvey as the first baseman of the Los Angeles Dodgers, prices were favorable to a family of four. A Dodger dog and Coke today costs over $12.

Going to see Wayne Gretzky of the Los Angeles Kings in the 1980s was a good time. Families could enjoy seeing this exciting team without breaking the bank, so to speak. Gretzky would go on to become one of the all-time greats of the NHL.

One time, Teresa went on a date to a Los Angeles Dodger game. She was screaming and yelling as much as any fan would carry on. The Dodgers were exciting to see. As the hits were added up and the scoring increased, so were the voices in the stands. We've all heard them on our television sets. It could become bedlam out there.

One man, in front of Teresa, was so engrossed with the woman behind him. He ended up in heated discussions wanting to know who she was and could he call her even though she was with a date.

That woman was, indeed, Teresa. When they finally were able to speak, they talked for a long while.

Teresa told him where she worked and what she did and discussed the driving she was required to do her job. He introduced himself as Kevin Warner. He was amazed at the driving time she spent. In doing so, he invited her to move into his home in Ontario, California. He had a couple of extra rooms in the back of his house. He discussed this even knowing he had a female roommate in his house.

Can one say, "I see trouble brewing"?

Oh, where were her angels when she accepted? They were still watching out for her. Jesus was still speaking constantly to her. However, Ontario, California, was only a half hour or so to her place of work in San Bernardino. She could cut the driving time by more than half and have more time with her children. It seemed like to a good choice to relocate. Again? It even looked good financially. The rent Kevin quoted was beyond more than reasonable.

Autumn was livid when she found out even though she was living with her aunt. She wanted nothing to do with this arrangement. Timmy was approaching his teens and more than rambunctious. He was hyperactive and couldn't sit still much less adhere to the rules of Kevin's house. Joey was an active little girl who really did for herself and went along with whatever mommy wanted.

Unfortunately, another mishap, more like a tragedy, hit Teresa. As she was having tests completed at the hospital where she worked, her doctor asked her to see a neurologist. He wanted to have X-rays done since her walking movements did not appear to his liking. After the x-rays were completed, the neurologist diagnosed Teresa with multiple sclerosis.

She needed to be put in a wheelchair to relieve the pressure on her back and her legs. This meant working was no longer feasible. With time, hopefully, there would be progress so that the pressure on her spine and legs would be alleviated and she could regain her movements.

As every incident for Teresa would be, this was not the short-term solution she had hoped. It also was not a positive outlook for

Kevin. Work stopped. The paychecks stopped. The bills increased and piled up. Life became desperate…again.

With all the stress, Kevin became another monster in Teresa's life. He wanted the camaraderie of a sports buddy. He wanted that experience he had at Dodgers Stadium. Since Teresa could not go to a sports venue at the moment, or any moment in the near future, he regarded his life first. Forget the fact that the health of someone he should have had feelings and concerns was the immediate issue. Kevin didn't want someone mooching on his back. He had his bills. Teresa was supposed to pay hers.

Since he also was a fanatic for all sports, he couldn't appreciate it when Teresa couldn't spend the "quality" time he wanted going to a game and whooping it up. Yelling at the TV was not the same. It became a burden.

On top of that, he hated Timmy but loved Joey. Kevin could stand the cute little girl who was just to herself. The hyperactive Timmy drove him crazy. It was the final straw when Timmy put his feet, with shoes, on the sofa and TV stand. He would drop food under the TV stand and wouldn't pick it up. Once was forgivable but not multiple times, after being warned and told to pick up his food. Kevin's place looked a mess and his tolerance was lost. The little male monster was a spoiled brat! Kevin had reached his boiling point and was going to do something about it.

The day Kevin Warner literally kicked Teresa and her children out of his house was a miserable day—miserable because it was pouring outside. Kevin didn't care about the rain or Teresa and the kids. They weren't his responsibility. He wanted his happy sports life back. He wanted the peace without a hyperactive kid.

Kevin Warner, in his selfish, egotistical life, threw out Teresa's family with no place to go. He did not think how a woman, now in a wheelchair with MS, with two children would manage. He didn't care! He never thought of the difficulties they would confront. He couldn't imagine the boomerang effects that could slap him in the face later in life. He probably never heard the saying "for every action, there is a reaction." Kevin was not Catholic!

While Teresa was with Kevin, for about a year, they attended Disciples of Christ Church. Teresa became quite friendly with many of those who attended the services. She actually was very popular since many could feel how close to God and Jesus Christ she was. When a person had that aura, one would want to be close and learn more.

Teresa tried, many times, to have Kevin take them to the Catholic Church in the area. He was having nothing to do with it. It was his church or nothing. Teresa knew that praying to God and Jesus was vitally important. If she couldn't do it in a Catholic Church, she would have to accept what was available. She knew that God and Jesus were guiding her in this direction at this moment for a reason.

Kevin, on the other hand, was nowhere near as spiritual a human being. He was thoughtless, uncaring, and insensitive. Teresa understood what would eventually become of the person known as Kevin Warner. At this moment, she didn't need to think about him. She needed to focus on the here and now.

They were now homeless with no money and no place to rest their bodies. She needed to get to a phone so she could call the church. She wanted a miracle of her own to manifest as quickly as possible.

CHAPTER 19

They did have a couple of umbrellas. BIG DEAL! With Teresa in a wheelchair, a couple of bags with a few clothes for each of them, they wheeled and walked to the nearest bus stop or overhead covering, whichever came first.

Normally when a family would go outside for an adventure, they're not thinking of doing it in the rain. Waiting and wondering where the nearest shelter could possibly be was difficult with two children hanging on and trying to navigate the surroundings. Going in reverse and knocking on Kevin's door was not an option. He didn't care about throwing them out in the rain. Why would he look at their drenched faces and care about them now?

It's not that Teresa didn't know Ontario, California. She had become familiar with the streets since she had driven them many times before being forced to stay in a wheelchair. What became mindboggling and stressful was the fact that they didn't have any money. It was raining. No! It was pouring. She reminded herself over and over that she had two children hanging on to her. She also needed to relax and pray.

One day, she thought. *God will remember the unfortunate individual known as Kevin Warner. I pray dear Lord Jesus for assistance and mercy.*

Then Timmy, out of the blue, noticed a man, in the rain, and staring at them. "Mom!" Timmy spoke loudly since the rain was drowning out his voice. "There's a man over there. He's looking at us. He wants to talk to you."

"What man?" Teresa asked him. "Where?"

"Across the street. He's waving at us."

Teresa turned her head in the opposite direction she was looking. Indeed, there was a man waving at her. She waited a few more minutes hoping the rain would subside a bit. She said a little prayer. Just as her thoughts had materialized in her head, the rain did stop. Teresa then took her children and maneuvered up the street toward the man. When she got close enough to talk with him, he totally surprised her.

"I've been waiting for you," he said.

"Waiting for me!" Teresa exclaimed. "How did you know I would be here?"

"How come you don't know the answer?" the man asked in a calm voice. "You of all people should know."

"My son said you want to talk with me."

"I do," the man stated. "I've been waiting for you," he said again. He then reached into his pockets and withdrew vouchers. Many vouchers! Enough vouchers to last for a few weeks' worth of hotels, restaurants, grocery stores, and stores to buy clothing and transportation needs.

"How? Why? I don't understand," Teresa muttered.

"How is it you don't understand?" the man asked. "You of all people! Didn't you die? Twice? Didn't you come back? Twice!" the man explained in the calmest of voice. "Why don't you know?" the man just stared at Teresa as she started tearing up.

Teresa's clothes, while not soaked, were dripping wet. Timmy and Joey's clothes were wet from the waist down as the umbrellas had protected parts of them. They continued to stare at the man while he continued.

"Don't you know that God provides for you?" the man questioned. "I knew you would be here with your children. The Son sent me to you."

Teresa stood dumbfounded. Wait! Correction! She *sat* dumbfounded in her wheelchair without saying a word. She looked at Timmy and Joey and smiled. Then she looked back at the man.

"Thank you," Teresa uttered softly.

"For what?" he asked as he took a cloth from his pocket and wiped his cheek. His clothing was as dry as just having been removed from the laundry drier.

"For this!" she pointed to the vouchers.

"This is nothing!" the man said. "You were told you were the first miracle. You were told that you would see more miracles. This is for you to open your eyes and realize. You were asked to pray. Pray often. Pray always. Pray for all. So start praying."

"I will," Teresa stated.

"By the way, you won't see me again. I've completed my task," the man said. He started to go since it was no longer raining. Although it would not have mattered if it was raining, it never affected the man.

"Don't forget to pray," he muttered again and began to leave.

As he turned to leave, Timmy looked up at the man eyeing his back. It was then that he saw the wings. They were beautifully white and long. They went down past his waste and moved in perfect unison with the man's strut.

Timmy's eyes widened. His mouth opened as large as it could. He wanted to say something but couldn't. At first he muttered under his breath that he saw an angel. Teresa looked at Timmy and Joey. She stared at the vouchers in her hand. Her head was fixated on her hand for only a few seconds before she realized the man was no longer around. She turned her head in every direction. He was gone.

"Did you see where he went?" she asked Timmy.

He just shook his head, smiled, and said "I saw the angel."

It was here and now that Teresa knew she had to change. With the rain having stopped and the sun beginning to peak through the clouds, Teresa and her children began to walk, and wheel, to the closest hotel. They would have a place to sleep for a few weeks. They would have food. There would be clothing that they could purchase.

It was this very moment that Teresa knew she would be going back to church on more than a regular basis. She didn't have to rely on Kevin Warner. She needed to rely on herself. Ontario, California would not just be a place to exist without purpose. She would establish herself within the church community and pray often, for everyone and always for herself and her children.

Teresa also realized that Jesus Christ had sent her back for not only one reason but also multiple reasons. She was to be the vessel to witness to many. She was to prove that with prayer, anything can happen—and "happen" for the good.

She would pray for anyone and everyone. She would reach out to as many as needed if only for a word of hope and faith. It was her faith that would be a catalyst for many to begin anew. They would realize that the words of God Almighty and Jesus Christ were there for all to revere and study. This would be Teresa's use of the second commandment and witness of "Loving Thy Neighbor…"

Going to church in Ontario, California, almost daily, began a drastic change. She did contact the Catholic Church in the area as well. Becoming a part of the church community gave her great confidence and the need to move forward. They gave her enough money to provide for an apartment, food, schooling for Timmy and Joey, and medical needs. The church reached out to many of the churches in the area. Miraculously, every one of the churches reached into their pockets and provided even more than she could have imagined.

People were willing to drive her wherever she needed to go. They assisted with Timmy and Joey if Teresa needed help. Meals were cooked. The apartment was cleaned. It was all for the grace of God and Jesus Christ that Teresa felt whole again. The Holy Ghost reached out and blew praises in every direction for Teresa and her children.

And oh how Teresa prayed. She prayed for the entire congregation and community. She proved the worthiness that was handed down to her and only voiced positive things every day. Her negativity, if she had any left within her, was gone. The wisdom bestowed on her was heard. They knew what had happened to her. They came to her help.

When Moses hit the rock and supplied water to the masses, they thanked God Almighty. It was another new reason to believe and stop complaining. Miracles occur for a reason and at a time when that miracle opens the minds of all those who doubt.

Not only was Teresa thanking all those who reached out to support her, but also they were showing the true meaning of heaven on earth. This was a society of believers giving praise to one of the needy souls. They all felt heaven-sent.

It was here that Teresa also found out that the doctor had misdiagnosed her with MS. She could get out of the wheelchair and be "free" again. She could stand and walk into the church and give praise without the crutch of a wheelchair. She could show those giving to her that the work she was told to do by Jesus Christ would be cemented in her mind, body, and "soul."

CHAPTER 20

After a year and also with the full support of her family helping her again, Teresa, Timmy, and Joey returned to Barstow. She hoped this would be her final move. Once again, her sisters reached out during the evening so Teresa could begin to live a new life with real friends. Autumn was also there and happy that her mother was in her life full time.

Teresa was able to work again. She was fully grounded and diligently went to church and prayed as she was told. She went up to those who needed a word of hope. She spoke to anyone whom she felt needed guidance and direction.

That smile she had once lost was brilliant again. That smile that came from within and knowing that Jesus Christ was directing her in all that she did beam brightly. Her angels were watching as she realized they had never left her.

Teresa could hit herself on the head with a hammer for losing that special glory Jesus Christ had given to her. She needed to put herself in Jesus's sandals and ask, "What would Jesus do?" With every forward movement, Teresa was to think about the miracle she was and ignite the light that shines on all.

Eventually, she hooked up with past high school buddies who inquired about her life. She went into a local bar in Barstow called David's Crazy Turtle. It was owned by a friend from high school. Her drink of choice was water in a tall glass with no ice.

At first there were the questions if she was sure water was all she wanted. Teresa knew what was going on inside the heads of those who would question. "Who goes into a bar and only orders water?"

Honestly? No one.

Teresa was still young, attractive, and had many men looking at her. It was the 1990s. Imagine some jerk announcing to his or her friend a new joke he made up and said, "A woman goes into a bar and sits on one of the stools. The bartender comes up to her and says, 'What'll you have good-looking?' The woman says, 'Water, no ice."

She then jokes, "I'm watching my weight."

The bartender just looked blindly at her and wondered if trouble followed her wherever she went. It was a good thing that Teresa knew David. They rehashed their high school days. Teresa asked when he acquired the bar. He asked if she still wanted to be a nurse or had indeed become one.

Oh, the stories that would fly by over the next hour or maybe two! How about over three! Teresa and David talked until it was time to close the bar. They both had a million questions on their minds. Reminiscing the old days of high school brought many terrific memories.

When David asked about Tim, Teresa just said he was persona non grata. He was out of her life after a lifetime of hell with two beautiful daughters and one son under her wings. She didn't go into the disease or the hospital at the time. That could be left for another night or many nights.

One time when Teresa was in the bar, as she had become a regular and was talking with other friends, did a problem arise. Sitting and minding their own businesses, they got up and started to dance to the music playing throughout the bar. The music was loud and the floor was crowded.

Someone went over to their table and decided to switch Teresa's drink with vodka. No one knew who switched the drinks or noticed when it had been switched. After a few dances and getting perspired and heated, they went back to the table. Teresa grabbed her glass and chugged its entire contents.

This, obviously, was not a good thing. Teresa's head began spinning. She was not used to drinking, she hadn't had a drink since before she had recovered from her disease, and she became sick. Then she felt an uncomfortable pain in her stomach. Finally, her stomach bounced and churned.

No sooner than one could possibly imagine, she raced toward the women's bathroom, threw the door open, and lunged for one of the toilets. Dropping her head into the top portion of the toilet, she vomited over and over.

A strange man—dressed in what seemed to be newly pressed khaki slacks with the seams ironed to the bottom of the legs, a white shirt that looked as if it had been expertly starched, and a blue sports jacket and black shoes that shined so bright it looked as if one could see their reflection in them—opened the door to the women's bathroom. Seeing Teresa on the floor and hurling everything in her stomach, he gently took her hair, which was exceptionally long and past her butt. He then held it in one of his hands so that nothing from her mouth would get into the hair.

He had seen the entire race to the bathroom. He had eyed Teresa before she raced into the bathroom. He didn't see anyone switch her drink. However, watching Teresa dance with her friends and seeing her long flowing hair bob back and forth made him want to know her.

Teresa was blind to the man and thought it was one of her friends. The fact that her hair was in his hands made no difference. She was still vomiting until nothing came out anymore. Then she began to dry heave. The feeling that your stomach would reach the top of your throat and then pour out of your mouth and blood would shoot into the toilet left Teresa even sicker.

She was dizzy. The room was spinning. She tried opening her eyes without feeling as if her head would fall farther into the toilet. This left her wanting to quit living just for that instance. While she didn't know for sure that the feeling would eventually fade, she had been informed many times by friends who had experienced this effect in the past.

When? That was another question that wouldn't be answered until later. WAY LATER! The man quickly turned, grabbed a paper towel, turned on the cold water, and soaked the paper towel. All this was done while he still had her hair in his hand. Taking the cold, wet paper towel, he began dabbing at Teresa's forehead. The coolness made Teresa stop dry heaving as she felt a calmness coming over her even though she was still dizzy.

The door to the bathroom slowly opened, and David peaked in first to see if anyone was in the bathroom. The hour was getting late, and he wanted to begin closing the bar. He had not seen Teresa rushing through the bar. Seeing a man in the women's restroom was awkward. Seeing a man in the women's restroom and recognizing that Teresa was there left him with a ton of questions and wanting to rush to grab the stranger. For some uncanny reason, David came in and stared at the stranger. He didn't grab him but saw that he was dabbing her face. He looked into the toilet, saw the spoils of Teresa's stomach, and quickly understood. The stranger lifted her head a few inches while David flushed the toilet and freshwater would enter the bowl. The coolness of the water flowing into the bowl also felt a bit refreshing to Teresa's face.

"Is she all right?" David asked.

"She seems to be calming down a bit," the strange man replied. "I saw her race into the bathroom and just knew it was not good." The man was correct.

Teresa was finally done vomiting her guts out. She was tired and very sleepy. Her head was tilted to the side, and she was almost passed out. She heard the voices and again determined it must be her friends.

At this point, David knew that Teresa did not drink. The strange man knew that getting her home was now priority number one. Priority number two was figuring out how to get her home and close the book on priority number one.

"I have to close the bar," David said. "Give me five, maybe ten minutes, and we'll take her home. I know where she lives."

"No problem. I'll wait here," the man stated.

David turned to leave and then turned around again to look at the man. "I've seen you before. Haven't I?"

"I've been in your bar a few times."

"Fort Irwin?" David asked.

"Yes, sir," the man replied.

"Thanks for helping out. I've known this woman for a long time. She's good people."

The man just nodded his head, watched David leave the bathroom, and proceeded to get Teresa off of the floor. She was out cold and breathing steadily.

CHAPTER 21

A few minutes passed just as David had said. By the time he came back into the bathroom, the man had Teresa standing up. He was also holding her to prevent her from falling.

Do you know that feeling when someone or two people are carrying you? They're holding you up without falling and proceeding to take you to your car? You're not consciously walking because you're sleeping, but deep inside you know you're moving.

Maybe the next day, you'll discern it in your mind and then ask questions. You'll have no idea how you got into your car and drove home. You want to know how or who got into your bed. That's exactly what happened, sort of.

David and the unnamed man put Teresa in her car. The man had originally taken a bus to get to the bar and would drive Teresa's car. David got into his car and drove to Teresa's home. Then they took Teresa out of the car, where David and the man were met by Autumn who was babysitting Timmy and Joey. Autumn opened the front door, and the two men ushered in.

Okay, ushered was too nice of a term because they half carried and half walked Teresa into her room without dropping her. Gently putting Teresa on her bed, they walked out of the room and told Autumn what had occurred but not the entire ordeal. Sometimes, too much information was really too much information, especially if you're the daughter of the person needing to get into bed. Just the fact that Teresa was home and safe was enough for now.

Everyone was tired and any questions could and would be left until the morning. Autumn was just glad her mother was safe, thanked both David, whom she knew, and the man, who remained nameless. They walked out of the house. Autumn closed the door.

David got into his car. The man stared at David walking to his car and then heard David's voice.

"Hey, man. Thanks again. There aren't too many who would go out of their way to do what you did."

"No problem, sir," the man said. "It was my pleasure."

"I didn't catch your name," David uttered.

"No, sir. I didn't give it," the man said. He watched as David started his car.

"Daniel, sir. Name's Daniel Van Earp."

Before David drove away, he asked, "How are you going to get to where you need to be?"

Dan quickly responded, "I'll call a taxi, sir. No problem."

David then left as the man just stood there.

Calling a taxi would mean walking to a place that was open and had a phone available. He did not want to knock on the door to the house since he figured it would look awkward asking to use a phone at the hour it was. Besides, Autumn was probably in her teens and would feel uncomfortable letting in a strange man even though he was one of two who helped her mom.

Nope! Walking and calling a taxi wouldn't work. Looking at his watch, that was obviously not going to happen. Daniel eyed the porch of Teresa's home and saw a couple of rattan chairs. Walking to the chairs, he sat down and got as comfortable as he could.

What he did do was wait. The nighttime would soon become dawn. The sun would come up as it did every morning. According to the weather conditions, no rain was forecast, which was very infrequent in Barstow. Daniel let his eyes doze off but only for a little while. He was used to getting little sleep.

When the next morning fully arrived, Teresa awakened with a monster headache. She gradually lifted herself off her bed and had the exact questions fully forecast earlier. She was still in the same clothes from last night. Grateful to be able to stand, Teresa walked into the bathroom and looked in the mirror. That was her first mistake. Then she turned on the light to the bathroom. That was her second mistake. She quickly closed her eyes and slowly opened them to let the light seep in slowly. She knew it was going to be a long day.

She didn't call out for anyone as she also knew her voice would ignite another pounding in her head.

Putting one foot gingerly in front of the other without tumbling over, she eventually reached the door to her room and opened it. She walked into the front room and eyed Autumn in the distant kitchen. The blinds to the living room were opened.

The glimmer of sun streaming through made her squint just enough to see the outside world. Teresa strained to look out toward the front yard. It was then she saw a strange man on the porch.

Going to the front door and opening it, Teresa walked out. The air was cool, but not cold. Seeing the man in one of the chairs, Daniel then opened his eyes and saw Teresa.

"I imagine you stayed here all night?"

"Yes, ma'am," Daniel said in an affirmative voice. "I wanted to make sure you were all right after your unfortunate episode."

"My unfortunate episode is a little blurry right now," Teresa replied and started to laugh, stopped quickly as the laugh made her head hurt. "I guess I owe you a lot."

"No, ma'am. You owe me nothing. By the way, my name is Daniel."

"Well, Daniel, I think I'm still Teresa. Would you like cup of coffee?"

"Thank you."

Teresa and Daniel, soon to be known to Teresa as Dan, went into the house. Autumn was still in the kitchen. She sized up Dan and said nothing. Teresa proceeded to make some coffee, gave Dan a cup, and started to leave the kitchen.

"I'm just going to clean up, wash my face, and change," Teresa muttered softly. "I'm sure you'll need to get back to wherever you need to be. I'll drive you."

"Thank you, ma'am," Dan said. "That's very kind of you."

"Kind of me?" Teresa proclaimed. "What you did for me last night was downright incredible." Then Teresa blurted out, "By the way, where do you live?"

"Fort Irwin, ma'am," Dan replied.

Teresa almost did a double take but then shook head. "Oh? Oh! Okay," and silently laughed to herself as she left the kitchen and excused herself. "Why am I not surprised?" she whispered.

Autumn looked at Dan and said nothing. She was standing next to one of the kitchen counters and was just off in her own world for the time being. She did not want to make Dan uncomfortable and knew that Fort Irwin was more than an hour away from where they lived. She also knew she would be babysitting her two siblings again while her mother drove "Ma'am Dan." At least he was polite.

CHAPTER 22

Daniel Van Earp was an army soldier stationed at Fort Irwin. He loved being in the military and wore his uniform with pride. His rank was listed as a "specialist" who trained and worked as a "smoker." This was an individual that trained soldiers to utilize generators in the creation of smoking out an area and to hide their tanks to camouflage from the enemy. It also aided in assisting troops when moving in a forward formation and protecting from enemy fire.

He was 5'1" in height and muscular-looking with dark, piercing brown eyes and wore BC glasses according to Teresa. They were issued by the military. He would joke that the glasses issued to him were BCG, an acronym for birth control glasses. They were thick and protected his eyes from possible damage.

His black hair was cut in typical military style but had some growth. His medium-sized hands were rough but gentle. His voice was never loud but firm. His movements were deliberate in that his training and job requirements needed him to be precise and direct. Working in the military and the arena of his job description, Daniel, or as he preferred sometimes to be called Dan, took his job as serious as anyone possibly could. He loved being in the military and loved his job.

He was responsible for making sure all soldiers understood the importance when going into battle. He was responsible for making sure they knew to protect their fellow soldiers. Dan took each one of their lives in his own hands and made them his children and his family.

"That's what we do. That's what I do," he would always say. He had Teresa's face imbedded in his mind the night he spent at her house outside on the porch. Her bloodshot, hazel eyes did sparkle as Dan knew that once the redness went away, they would melt his heart. Her long light-brown hair was loose when he held it in his hands. But he knew that once Teresa let it hang in the wind, it would flow like those of a model for a shampoo commercial. He could feel the touch of her hands in his and wanted to protect every inch of her.

After Teresa came out of her room and back into the kitchen, Dan could see that her eyes were sparkling, hazel green. No red. Her long light-brown hair flowed, as he thought it would.

"Okay," Teresa said. "I'm ready."

"Thank you, again," Dan said as they walked out of the kitchen, out of the house, and into Teresa's car.

As they were pulling onto the road, Dan asked if she were hungry because he was. They stopped at a fast-food restaurant drive-through and ordered breakfast sandwiches and coffee. Driving onto I-15 N, they headed for the first exit after getting out of Barstow. A few minutes later, they were driving the twenty-six miles to Fort Irwin.

"I actually saw what happened last night as you were rushing into the bathroom," Dan admitted. "I didn't see who switched your glasses, but after you raced toward the bathroom, I had a feeling it was not going to be for the usual reason."

"I'm just so glad you were there," Teresa uttered. "Do you normally watch for women rushing to the bathroom?" She then smiled and laughed.

Dan looked at Teresa, took a bite of his breakfast sandwich, and smiled. "Actually, I'm always very observant. It's part of my job on the Army base. When I get a chance to wind down after work, I usually take the bus to Barstow and spend time with some of the others in my unit. We like to laugh, have a few drinks, and relax. If we find a woman having too much to drink, falling flat on her feet on the dance floor, or rushing to the bathroom, we decide whose turn it is to rescue the woman."

Teresa looked at Dan while trying not to get into an accident on the two-lane road to Fort Irwin. The look on her face was one of astonishment.

"Relax," Dan said. "I'm only joking." Dan smiled. "Doing what I did was not the norm for me. I'm usually very reserved. Being with a bunch of men all the time does lead to many jokes. Seeing what happened to you really bothered me. I just wish I knew who did it."

"Huh?" Teresa just continued to drive and took a bite out her sandwich.

"I do hope I haven't offended you in any way," Dan then said.

"No offense taken," Teresa shot back. "It's been some time before a man picked me off of the bathroom floor, wiped my mouth, and drove me home. I figured this time I'll get someone from the military." Dan looked at Teresa and started to laugh.

"Good one," he lamented. "It's nice to hear a woman shoot the bull back. I deserved that."

"You're not the only one who knows how to tease."

The next thirty minutes or so were spent telling each other about the other, going over their lives, asking questions, and receiving funny answers or real ones. They had a great time and felt totally at ease. Dan explained to Teresa that his full name meant that he was the "son of Earp." Yep! That son of Earp.

Daniel Van Earp was an adopted great grandson of the famous sheriff, gunslinger, and frontiersman, Wyatt Earp. He would often have to explain his last name since almost everyone he met knew the stories of his great grandfather who was best known for his involvement at the OK Corral and many other escapades.

"What about the adopted?" Teresa wanted to know. She could obviously see that Dan was Asian.

"I was adopted at an early age," Dan explained. "I'm of a Vietnamese descent. I grew up in Ohio and then entered the military to get away from the family."

While very proud of his family's past notoriety, Dan wanted to move beyond this. He was actually molested as a boy by his father. Dan wanted to protect his sisters from the monster in his house. When it was time to leave, he enlisted to get away. He now only wanted to make his own history and "escapades."

Sometimes it becomes trite to have to explain, over and over, who he is and that people should look at him and not either put him on a pedestal or down because he was adopted. He did revere the stories of the past as Dan was proud. However, this was the late 1990s. The Wild West was over, and the only gun he carried was when he was on base. Eventually the conversation led to discussions of family background on Teresa's side since Dan had already discussed his family background. Teresa did go into her previous marriage and her children, sisters, and brothers and her disease.

She explained why, for the time being, water was her choice of beverage. She was actually on medication. She did enjoy a glass of wine, or other, in the past. Only for a little while longer did she need the medication.

Then Teresa mentioned her spiritual preferences to Catholicism. She informed Dan she enjoyed going to Mass, receiving the Eucharist, and praying for others. It was her mission. God Almighty, Jesus Christ, and the Holy Ghost were first and foremost.

"So this Catholicism," Dan said, "is this something you've had your entire life? I mean, you've been through a lot."

"This Catholicism?" Teresa chimed in not knowing if she should laugh or wince.

"Yeah! Let's look at it again," Dan continued while smiling the entire time. "You were married. You have two daughters and one son. You had the marriage annulled because it wasn't in the Catholic Church. You met Jesus and he showed you the rooms of all three levels…"

"What? Rooms?" Teresa couldn't believe what he was saying while she was smiling and knowing he could, again, be joking or not! He saw that she was starting to feel a bit uncomfortable. Also, she was still driving. Getting into an accident was not on the agenda.

"I apologize. I'm just pulling your leg, again. Just because I'm in the military doesn't mean I'm not a believer. I grew up going to church every week, but at a Protestant church."

Teresa's posture relaxed as she realized he enjoyed a good bit of teasing and tried to advance the conversation. The smile on his face was charming and fragile at the same time. She knew he wanted to be with her. She could hear her angels speaking to her as they did approve. She also knew they were telling her to watch the road.

"Teresa, I'm an individual who must perform the duties to protect many with the instructions provided by my superiors. I need to let go after the day so I can wake up and do the same thing the following day. I guess that includes joking around and relieving any stress." Dan was staring at Teresa. "Please forgive me for the ill-timed abrupt statements. Without a higher understanding of God, I'm not sure I could proceed to do my work. Remember, I swore an oath to my country and also to God."

Teresa started to laugh to herself and then out loud. She pointed a relaxed finger in his direction. "You sound just like one of those recruiting soldiers in the commercials."

Assuring her that he meant only to be funny, he said if she weren't driving, he would want to kiss her. Teresa only replied that when the car stopped, she would gladly accept that invitation.

"By the way, did I tell you my age? I'm only nineteen."

"What?" Teresa looked at Dan with total surprise.

"Just kidding! Again. I wanted to see the look on your face."

The drive eventually came to an end at the entrance to Fort Irwin. Even though Dan had the credentials to be there, Teresa would need to park the car, get out, and register the car and herself inside the office area. Dan obviously went with her to validate Teresa.

While this didn't take long, by the time Teresa had completed with the registration and picture taking, the men inside doing the checking and registration were calling Dan by a new name. Funny as it was, "Teresa Dan" now stuck for a while. Teresa and Teresa Dan got back into the car. Dan directed her to where he lived.

"May I see you again?" he asked as he started getting out of the car.

"I don't know," Teresa shot back. "I'm not used to being with a man so much younger than me." She then laughed. "I wouldn't want someone telling me I'm robbing the cradle."

Dan leaned over and gave Teresa a huge kiss. When he pulled away, he smiled.

"Even if the younger man kissed like that?"

"Soldier boy! You can do that whenever you want."

Before Dan exited the car, he gave Teresa his phone number. All he needed to do was look up her information in the records she provided when registering.

"I'll see you soon," he reassured her.

"Not before I see you first," Teresa stated and drove off.

CHAPTER 23

It was as little as a month. Teresa knew how she felt. Dan knew he had met the woman of his dreams. It made no difference to Teresa that she was seven years older than Dan. He was smart, handsome, funny, and responsible had a good job and knew what he wanted to do and where he wanted to move into the future.

"But only a month?"

Autumn, Teresa's oldest daughter, was against the marriage. It was too soon. Moving too fast as she would consistently voice. Autumn didn't want anything to do with someone who would be her "step." She had been taking care of her siblings for some time while mom went partying and trying to "find" herself.

"Hasn't she learned from her past mistakes?" Autumn would think to herself.

Teresa's mother was definitely in favor of it as she liked Dan. He treated her well. After the nightmare of her previous marriage and the huge mistake she made with her previous relationship, she was happy that Teresa found an individual who respected her identity and did not want to control her. Dan was certainly not a chauvinist, a manipulator, or a sinner but an individualist who believed that marriage was a bond for two to work together.

Dan also wanted to be supportive within the Catholic Church. He would attend Mass every Sunday at Fort Irwin with Teresa and the girls. Knowing that Teresa was guided by Jesus Christ and many angels, he understood the importance of being grounded in HIS teachings. He knew that with Teresa in his life, she would not only be his equal but also broaden his knowledge of God and Jesus Christ.

Before they married, Dan informed Teresa that he wanted to eventually leave the military early and would be applying for a position in New York on Long Island. He had his choice of two jobs. One was in business. The other was in security. He explained that once they were married, the military would move the family to the destination of their choice.

Dan knew it was fast, but he also knew he loved her. He wanted to take care of Teresa and her children. He would be the father they never had and would never think to raise a finger in their direction, or any direction for that matter, that would cause them any harm.

As for Teresa, the derogatory term used by Tim would never be uttered by Dan. There were plenty of other "loving" terms he preferred to use. He also would never think of being disrespectful to her.

Teresa knew Dan was everything Tim had never been. He treated her well, and she truly loved him as much as he loved her. When they were apart, it felt like a knife was cutting into her heart. She was listening to the voices in her head and they approved. The only snag was they were proceeding without getting married in the church.

They all piled into their car and drove to Las Vegas. It was easy to get a license without waiting or blood tests, as was the normal procedures in many other states, cities, or towns, you name it. Saying their vows before a marriage officiant, an individual licensed in Nevada and authorized by the clerk of Clark County, Teresa and Dan tied the knot. And it was not by Elvis.

Teresa, Autumn, Timmy, and Joey then moved to Fort Irwin. She knew Fort Irwin would not last a long time. Once married, all of the necessary plans were discussed in detail for the move to Long Island.

It had been a long time since she had been in her old stomping ground. She had left when she was six. Teresa did not even know if she would recognize any of it. Then again, who really would remember everything about where they lived at six years old? It was beginning to feel like déjà vu in that Teresa, along with her children, would be moving without Dan. They had already moved from Needles to Barstow, Barstow to Ontario, Ontario back to Barstow, and now to Fort Irwin. Soon it would be Fort Irwin to Long Island. Hopefully, this would finally be the last time.

Whether Teresa had discussed her early childhood did not matter to Autumn. As long as her mother and siblings were with her, she knew, as the oldest child, that she would have the first opinion should another major interruption take place. The first positive thing with the move was that her father would be out of their lives. It would be a long while before Autumn wanted to contact him.

The move to Long Island went without any problems. Dan already applied for early release from his tour of duty. It would only be a couple of months before he met them in their new home. Teresa and the girls had to move first. They had to find a place to live, schools to enroll and attend, and all the other responsibilities required when setting up in a new city or town. With the military moving them, it was surprisingly easy.

Even though money was tight, Dan and Teresa set up a joint account. Teresa was also exceptionally honest. She had to be. With Jesus and her angels talking with her daily, anything out of the ordinary would be met with constant silent discussions within herself. No one could interrupt her since she couldn't hear the outside world anyway. The good news? There were also daily conversations with Dan.

To say that Long Island had changed from the last time Teresa was there, in the 1960s, would be an understatement. The entire island was about 120 miles long and twenty-three miles in width. It was partitioned into two counties, Nassau and Suffolk. Nassau was considered the northern side and Suffolk is the southern. The population alone more than doubled in twenty-plus years. The Hamptons grew tremendously and became THE hub for the rich, famous, and infamous. Today, many private and expensive estates filled the Hamptons as the beaches were some of the best in the world. Many movies had been filmed along the Hamptons and the entire Long Island. Some of the most famous included *The Amityville Horror, Annie Hall, The Godfather,* and *Sabrina.*

F. Scott Fitzgerald, the famous writer, lived in Great Neck, also called West Egg, on Gateway Drive in Nassau County. The Great Gatsby, which told of the times of tremendous parties and included huge amounts of liquor, drugs, and bootlegging, was depicted by

Fitzgerald. For the purposes of privacy, since he was continuously interrupted, The Great Gatsby was completed in France on the French Riviera.

Teresa and her children settled in the village of Mastic Beach in 1990, which was in Suffolk County. It is south of Sunrise Highway, New York state Route 80, and lies just inland off the water. Mastic Beach is considered a Hamlet and a "census-designated place (CDP)" in the southeastern part of the town of Brookhaven.

Further history states that Mastic, which is slightly north of Mastic Beach, was originally named Forge until the late 1800s. The Long Island Rail Road built a station in 1882. A person can actually take the train into New York City. The Poospatuck Reservation is entirely within the community near the southern end of Mastic, which runs along the Forge River. Hence, the original name of Forge.

While waiting for Dan to get out of the military, which would not be for a couple of months, Teresa and the girls set up their new home in a rented house two blocks from where her mother now lived and began living a better life. While certainly not rich or even middle class, they were able to afford many things they previously couldn't on Dan's Army salary. Also with the help of local charities, Teresa was able to make a difference in the lives of her children.

Two months was approaching quickly as each day seemed like an eternity. Dan was readying to leave Fort Irwin and be with his family. Before he knew it, there was only one week left. He spoke with Teresa on the phone and said he expected to be with her by the end of the week. He would make sure their future was even brighter.

Dan was traveling on the rough terrain back to the main area of Fort Irwin. He was driving a Hummer with a smoke generator on the back of the Hummer as was his normal routine. His usual speed was that designated by the military, which was approximately twenty to thirty miles per hour.

The area at Fort Irwin was chosen strictly for one main reason. It was in the high desert area of California where all situations met whatever the world arenas would require should deployment throughout the world be necessary. The terrain at Fort Irwin could be rough and rugged. It was perfect for training when soldiers needed to go to the Middle East for combat. In the summer, it would get well over 100 degrees. In the winter, it could drop down to the thirties.

Fort Irwin was immense and could house and hold as many as 500,000 soldiers. Every soldier was expected to weather any temperature and endure all procedures during their training. Training would last for as long as a tour of duty or longer. Whether hilly terrain or not, driving could always be difficult, and great care was expected. Going down a rough hill was just as hard as going up.

The Hummer vehicle, with the smoke generator, leaned to one side. A new recruit was coming from the other direction into the field on the exit dirt road. Dan was coming out onto the same road. When he saw the other Hummer, he swerved to miss him. The smoke generator, being as heavy as it was, began causing Dan's Hummer to roll.

As hard as it was for Dan to try and compensate for the rolling of his vehicle, he could not stop the motion before it actually began. Dan's Hummer rolled. He couldn't get the door opened and felt the impact. It didn't take long before Dan's vehicle crushed him, killing him instantly.

Putting his Hummer in park and pushing on the emergency brake pedals, the other soldier rushed out and ran to Dan. He called out and heard nothing. He went to the driver's side trying to get a view of Dan to see if he was even conscious. Reaching for his radio, the soldier called for help. Time was of the essence. Emergency vehicles needed to be there now.

CHAPTER 24

It was a nice day. Teresa was technically alone in the home. Autumn and Timmy were at school, and the youngest, Joey, was playing in her room. Autumn and Timmy would be home in a couple of hours. Teresa had a glass of iced tea in her hands and was enjoying the early afternoon. It was peaceful in Mastic Beach.

Her mother lived several blocks away as she had finally had enough of her husband after thirty-two years. It was a constant battle of not knowing her husband was suffering from bipolar depression and taking it out on her. One day, he was great, and the next day, he was miserable. The following day was full of depression with anger and accusatory language. It was no wonder she got an annulment, moved to Mastic Beach, and ended up marrying her childhood sweetheart.

According to Teresa, it kind of "killed us kids." Her siblings were totally unaware of what was going on since they all had their own lives. No one knew that their father had such a disease. Bipolar depression had not been fully diagnosed, explained, or even studied in great detail in the 1970s or 1980s. Teresa explained, "It split us into 'his side versus her side.'" Her mother left their father, Teresa, and her siblings and headed for Long Island in 1983.

A knock came on Teresa's front door. She strolled to the door, gently opened it, and saw a military man standing outside through the screen door. He informed her that he was from Fort Hamilton. He had a folder under his arm.

"Ma'am," the soldier said. "Are you Mrs. Teresa Earp?"

Teresa looked at the man in the uniform and had a strange thought. What a great sound that was—Mrs. Teresa Earp. It rang well in her mind. She brought herself back to the man at her door.

"I'm sorry. Yes, I'm Teresa Earp."

"Ma'am," the soldier said, "may I come inside? It's about your husband."

"Oh!" Teresa replied. "My husband's not here right now. He's expected to be here at the end of the week."

"That's why I would like to come in, ma'am," the man said.

"I remember Dan always joking and calling me ma'am," Teresa explained. "I thought it was so formal. I remember him saying it was a military thing. You're always so formal. Would you like a cup of coffee or some water?"

"No, thank you, ma'am. I would like to come in and speak with you," the soldier said.

Teresa opened the screen door and let the man in. He walked into the front room, stood straight, and looked at Teresa with a serious look on his face.

"Would you like a glass of water? With or without ice?" Teresa asked starting to laugh and remembering that she had to order that drink for a while after her surgery. It was a standard joke for Dan and her when she explained that to uniformed soldiers. She started to go to the kitchen before the man stopped her.

"Ma'am? Please," he said. "I need you to listen to me."

"Of course," Teresa replied. She was smiling thinking of Dan and believing this was one of his jokes. She and Dan were always joking.

"Please listen to me," the soldier said. "This has to do with your husband as he won't be arriving at the end of the week."

"Of course he will!" Teresa exclaimed. "I just spoke with him a couple of days ago. He said he was getting out by the end of the week and would be here. He even contacted some friends at Fort Hamilton to let them know.

"Would you like to sit down please?" the man said. "I do not have good news, and it concerns your husband."

"What?!" Teresa said as she stood before the man still smiling.

"The United States of America and the president of the United States and the United States Army regret to inform you that your husband, Specialist Daniel V. Earp, has been killed in a military vehicle mishap out in Fort Irwin, which led to his untimely death."

Teresa looked at the man and thought it was one of Dan's jokes. She smacked his chest.

"Yeah? Okay. Is Dan outside?" she said as she started for the door. The man finally caught Teresa's arm and pulled her back into the room.

"This is not a joke. Here are the documents. Please understand. I'm sorry!"

When Teresa finally saw the papers, she looked at the officer in her living room. She looked again at the papers and fainted. The soldier caught hold of Teresa before she hit the floor. Laying her on the couch, he looked at his papers and saw that Teresa's mother was also a "next of kin." Her phone had been listed, and he called her using the phone in Teresa's kitchen. This was something the soldier had experienced many times in the past. It was never an easy procedure and was always heart-wrenching watching the bereaved hearing the untimely news. However, this was his job. He did it with stoic professionalism and would stay with Teresa until her mother showed up. The two could then calm her down should she become hysterical, and he needed to provide them with further information.

Teresa's mother was also very upset hearing the news. Not only was she happy that Teresa found true love, a man who treated her with such respect and compassion, but also she loved Dan. He always had the best intentions for the entire family and wanted a lifetime with them.

Even Autumn had changed toward Dan. She saw the way he looked at her mother. The short amount of time they had lived at Fort Irwin was nothing but happy moments for the entire family. They lived. They laughed. They conversed about everything and anything. Teresa and Dan spoke about the future and the plans to have an even better life on Long Island. Once they moved to Long Island, life did change. The schools were great!

Autumn made many friends. She didn't hear terrible things being said to her mom, and she saw the laughter and ease with which her mother felt about the family, her new husband, and her dad. While Autumn never called Dan "Dad," she just loved him.

After Dan was buried with full honors, it took a little while for everything to settle down. The darkness of the days that hung over the family didn't subside for what seemed like months. However, within a couple of weeks, Teresa and her daughters' lives changed dramatically.

She knew Dan had an insurance policy. In addition to receiving military benefits and disability, Teresa found out that Dan had doubled the insurance policy value. It was something that Dan had never discussed. It didn't cost that much extra on the policy and would definitely come in handy should some unfortunate event take place. Who knew or could predict the future? One might think a little hindsight would go a long way. This was not something to ever think about, but only something to be prepared for as Dan was always prepared.

Teresa now had some money that she had never had even when married to Tim. She was able to purchase a house in Mastic Beach. Her children were provided with their own rooms, and the space gave them the freedom they had never felt. Life moved along without the pallor appearances previously described.

Growing up was now happy and joyful. New experiences and opportunities were realized with each year. Timmy was able to be schooled at a private Catholic high school. College was paid in full for Autumn. Memories became ones to relive with smiles and laughter. The future became brighter for all of them. Even Fred, Teresa's brother, moved back to Long Island. Her sister Mary moved to Shirley, Long Island, from California as well. Shirley is actually a small town within the Mastic area. She was only a mile and half from Teresa.

Inside what was really only a few years, Teresa humbled herself in her new home and let her thoughts quickly reminisce on her past. Where had all the time gone? She was approaching the end of her thirties. It was as if a large merry-go-round was spinning and each 360-degree turn became a new episode in "the Life of Teresa-Rose Earp! A new season is coming soon."

All, kidding aside, Teresa was now firmly planted on Long Island, having started in Brooklyn and then moving to Long Island. At six, the family packed and moved to Central California. She married Tim after high school, worked in her desired field, and had children.

Tim then had the family move to Needles. She grew deathly ill, died, and saw Jesus Christ. The Holy Ghost breathed life back into her after an impossible three hours and twenty minutes. Jesus said she would be the first miracle. She moved from Needles back to Barstow. Teresa divorced Tim who then left after having met a "girl." He married her only because she became pregnant. It sounds like Tim never truly matured. Teresa again worked as a nurse and, due to her fanaticism with sports, met another "loser," Kevin. After moving in with Kevin in Ontario, California, and being misdiagnosed with MS, she and her family were thrown into the boiling pot of homelessness when Kevin could no longer stomach Teresa's maladies and Timmy's hyperactivities.

Joey, it seemed, was just going along for the ride since she was still too young to really understand. Family was all she needed. As long as she was with her mother, Joey knew she would be content, even if she didn't understand the word.

Walking in the rain and not "Singing in the Rain" with Timmy and Joey brought her to an angel. To this day, she still did not know the name of this wonderful angel but knew she was being led to a new life. That new life brought her back to the church and then back to Barstow.

She then met Dan where life took a wonderful turn to true love and marriage that would hopefully last a lifetime. Unfortunately, that lifetime didn't last as long as she would have wanted. Having relocated to Long Island, where she would learn of Dan's untimely death, she was now firmly planted in her own house without a mortgage.

She had her own fully paid vehicle, and her children were educated with all the bills having been paid by her husband's pensions and her disability. Dan would certainly be proud. According to Teresa, he was proud. He would communicate with her often.

If one were to hear the entire history, that person might not believe it. If a person were to write a book, then maybe many would come to know how truly blessed Teresa-Rose Earp was and is. After all, who could really come up with all of this besides God Almighty and Jesus Christ? If a movie were ever to be made, the title might be "A Fictional Tale in the Life of a Blessed Woman?"

However, this is not fiction. This is real. And the story is still not complete. Why? It's quite simple. The answer is because Teresa-Rose Earp's life is not done. There is another man in her life. There's another relocation to another state. The merry-go-round still has not stopped.

CHAPTER 25

Remember that Teresa was, and still is, a sports fanatic. Living on Long Island presented her with many teams to cheer. There was a sports bar and grill not far from her home called the Sports Page.

Teresa spent many hours watching the numerous televisions in the bar enjoying the Yankees or Mets for baseball. Then there were the Giants or Jets for football. Added to that were the Knickerbockers, or Knicks, for basketball and the Rangers and Islanders for ice hockey.

However, she was still an avid Los Angeles Kings fan. Meeting Wayne Gretzky was one of the highlights of her life. He even signed her ticket stub. Although the Kings never won the Stanley Cup during his tenure with the team, Gretzky would always be considered one of the greatest players in professional hockey. It really didn't matter which team she was rooting for. Whether American or National League for baseball, NFL or AFL for football, or the NBA or the NHL, all the teams were entertaining. She could yell at one particular game one hour and then switch allegiance to another team the next. The only real question of allegiance was that she now lived in the state of New York. It was New York or bust!

With Autumn and Timmy past the age of needing a babysitter and in high school or college, all that was left was Joey who was also growing quickly. Teresa spent a great deal of time enjoying the New York scene of sports. The Sports Page became the place where anyone who knew Teresa also knew where to find her if she needed to be found. She would go with her brother Ricky (real name was Fred), for company mainly for Monday night football.

As previously stated, another perk for Teresa was Dan's insurance and the monthly Army check she received due to his death. She stated that she could feel the presence of Dan at different moments in her life. The love he felt for her was enormous. He would make sure that she was able to afford many things she couldn't in the past. One of those perks was her ability to decorate her home in the Asian décor she preferred.

She always wanted this while in California but could never afford it. Thank you, Dan! Teresa was also, and still is, an attractive woman. Even with all the traumas she experienced in her life, she knew not to go to the bar without making herself presentable. Her eyes still dazzled bright hazel green. Her smile still showed a full set of beautiful teeth. Her hair still hung down in long tresses. She was a woman who many men would eye but rarely got up the nerve to introduce themselves.

This happens so often with men. They liked to talk a good game, excuse the pun, but it would sometimes take a lot of nerve, and liquor, to get the testosterone flowing and say a simple hello. Most women would actually like a gentleman to come and introduce themselves. The world was just so filled with nonsensical innuendos that sometimes nothing would get accomplished.

There was one group of such men who frequently saw Teresa. In that group was one man who was quite shy. In fact, he admitted to his friends that he had never had a girlfriend. After getting battered with the usual comments from his friends, they convinced him to get up the nerve and walk over to the table where she sat. Let's be frank about this. The man was not in high school. He was attending college for mechanical engineering. He was also taking courses in aeronautical engineering. Afterward, he would work for Izumi in the engineering department. It was a die-casting corporation that made steering wheels. He later would be working for other engineering firms.

He was not a child or a lovestruck teenager. He just happened to be a shy, sensitive individual who let life pass him by. He was studious and wanted a solid career. Dating was not a part of his plan. When he saw Teresa, the lightning bolt hit.

He just never understood the protocol for asking a woman out on a date or even getting into a serious conversation. To say he was nervous would be an understatement. He was the kind of gentle guy who always kept quiet and never said a word unless spoken to or had something to say. As he approached the table where Teresa sat with her brother Ricky, he leaned over to him.

"Excuse me," he said. "My name is John Maldonado. Would it be all right if I talked with the woman your with?"

Ricky could have played this for all it's worth. He could have said, "That's my date buddy. Want to go outside and do something about it?" Instead, Ricky simply said, "Of course you can." Ricky looked at Teresa and smiled. "She's right here and she has a mouth. Go for it." He turned and winked at his sister. "By the way, I'm her brother so don't worry. She's not my date. Have at it!" Ricky then picked himself up and went to the bar for a drink.

John slowly sat down and introduced himself. "My name is John Maldonado."

Teresa did take a small jab at the introduction. "I heard you say that to my brother."

"I've seen you here many times and wanted to get to know you. I just didn't know what to say."

Teresa just smiled at first. She thought that John was quite precious at first. "I'm Teresa. It's nice to meet you."

John was, indeed, shy a bit. He stood 5'8" tall, had dark-brown eyes, black hair, a medium build, and a wonderful angelic slightly rounded face. His voice was soft. Teresa obviously saw something wonderful in John Maldonado because the conversation lasted longer than the original game they were watching. Since John also enjoyed sports, they watched and conversed for quite some time. Things were going so well that when it was time to leave, he said he hoped to see her again.

That's it! Teresa thought. *Hoped to see me again?* she continued thinking and not believing that he didn't ask her for her number. And yet Teresa knew not to be too upset. In fact, she just smiled that simple smile she always gave and laughed under her breath. She knew John would eventually ask. In fact, it took two weeks before John got up the nerve to ask Teresa for a date. It's not that Teresa didn't eventually give John her phone number. And it wasn't a dinner date. It wasn't a date to go to a movie. It was a lunch date.

When they saw each other again at the Sports Page, it was a bit awkward…for John. They were having a drink, and he blurted it out.

"I honestly don't know how to do this?" he admitted.

"Do what?" Teresa asked. She was not going to just give in as it was slightly humorous to her.

"You know! I want to ask you out."

"So ask," Teresa replied in her quirky way.

"I just did," John mumbled back.

"Did what?" Teresa played.

John took a brief pause and a long breath. "I'm sorry, Teresa. I've never had a girlfriend before. This is a bit awkward for me."

"You think?" Teresa shot back with a bit of a smile as the twinkle in her eyes grew.

"I like you. A lot!" John shyly admitted. "I know we've only spoken a few times, but I like you a lot. I was hoping you would accept my invitation to go out to lunch."

"Let me think on that for a second," Teresa shot back. Her mind was going, *Lunch? Who asks a person to go on a date for lunch?* Then she saw John's face and immediately replied, "Okay! Second's up!"

John was, at first, a bit confused because he really didn't know Teresa's sense of humor in full. After all, they had just been seeing each other at the Sports Page. It was always sports conversations and slight small talk. It had never become serious to the point that she felt he would ever ask her out. It was always a good evening with a drink in hand and back-and-forth banter. They would watch their heads turning toward one television and then to another of whatever game would be playing.

In actuality, Teresa was also hesitant to go out on a date. After all, she was a widow with three children. Would there really be a man wanting a woman with this much "baggage?" She also had not been on a date with any man since Dan's death. She enjoyed having a good time at the Sports Page. It was on her terms. She could set whatever rules she wanted because of her situation. But she never expected this. She knew there would be good conversations with others who enjoyed watching sports as much as she did.

Okay, she said to herself. *Stop prosecuting yourself and realize that you have a right to enjoy yourself with another from the opposite sex. It was normal. Time had passed.*

Then Teresa added to her thoughts that Dan would want her to be happy. He would want her to move on and put the past behind her. Besides, she now had enough funds to enjoy her life as long as it was thumbs-up with her conversations with Jesus Christ.

"Can I ask you a question?" Teresa looked up to where John was sitting.

"Of course!"

"I need to let you know a couple of things before we do get together for lunch," Teresa blurted out.

"Ask away," John responded. "I'll answer as honestly as I can." John then waited for Teresa to ask or blurt out whatever she would say. Teresa started and then stopped. She was thinking that maybe they should meet for lunch first and discuss her thoughts while they ate.

"Teresa?" John questioned.

"Yes," she replied.

"Are you going to ask a question?"

She looked into John's eyes and quickly spoke. "Where did you want to meet for lunch?"

John was staring back at Teresa and knew that was not the question she really wanted to ask. However, instead of pushing the issue, he suggested one of a few different places. Teresa just picked one of the places he suggested and asked when. John replied that the weekend would be great, and he could pick her up.

"I need you to know that I'm a widow," Teresa shot out.

John blinked a bit dumbfounded. "Okay," he responded. "Anything else?"

"I have three children."

"Okay…"

"And…I know it's a lot to digest," Teresa explained. "I don't know many men who would want to go out with a woman with this much on her plate."

"Well," John muttered softly. "I don't believe that I should be put in the same category with 'many men,' and I'm asking you out because I like you. It shouldn't matter what your past was if you voice your concerns and I answer your questions."

Teresa was definitely liking John even more than just one minute ago. She knew this was going to go well.

"So did you want to meet at the restaurant or should I have the pleasure of picking you up?"

"You may have the pleasure," Teresa replied and gave John her address

CHAPTER 26

Not only did lunch go very well, but also Teresa was dropped off at her home, closed the door, and knew that John was the one. How did she know?

"Oh ye of little faith!"

Kindly remember that Teresa always knew, almost immediately, what life would have in store for her. Her experiences in the past were always solidified through her conversations with Jesus and her inner womanly intuition. Remember that brainiac mind? It was also filled with ESP—and not ESPN the sports network.

Teresa instinctively knew many of the things that would occur in her life. Looking back on her past, Teresa knew Tim was the one in high school. He hadn't shown any of the outrageous and disgusting qualities he possessed until after they were married and after the birth of Autumn. He was always kind and considerate and seemed to know what he wanted after the high school experiences were over and real life began. How could anyone possibly know that Tim would do a 180 degree and become the monster he ended up being?

We'll leave Kevin out of the equation. Kevin was just a selfish, self-centered egotistical monster who didn't deserve more of the written word.

Teresa knew that Dan was exceptional. His qualities of loyalty to his country and love for the woman in his life were beyond question. He knew he wanted to be married for the rest of his life to Teresa. He would never ever think of cheating on her or calling her obscene names. He knew he could be the father to Autumn, Timmy, and Joey that Tim never exhibited. Unfortunately, it would never fully materialize.

And finally, after the first date with John, she knew he was the one. Even though John was very reserved and quiet with his feelings, he was so enamored with Teresa. He could feel himself radiating inside. He would go to bed thinking of Teresa and couldn't wait for the next time they would see each other. She made him feel quite special.

They went to Yankee Stadium, Shea Stadium for the Mets, Madison Square Garden for both the Knicks and the Rangers, and Nassau Coliseum for the Islanders. They not only enjoyed lunch but also frequented with dinner reservations. They became inseparable.

Soon John graduated from college and began working in different engineering firms before landing at Izumi, a die-casting corporation. Even though the job brought in a good paycheck and security, he knew he wanted to work for the government. He informed Teresa that he was putting in applications at different locations on Long Island.

Meanwhile, on the romance side of life, Teresa introduced John to her children who were no longer children. They were full-grown young adults and teenagers with their own minds and opinions. As fortune would have it, they all liked John. As long as their mother was happy and he made her happier, they were fine with the relationship. Dan was also happy. He would contact Teresa and let her know how pleased he was that she was moving on. Life should be lived to its fullest.

On February 2, 2002, on the same day as Teresa's birthday and the Presentation of the Lord, Teresa and John were married at St. Andrews Episcopal Church. There were two prime reasons for getting married in the church as opposed to a civil marriage as Teresa had done before.

The first was that Teresa wanted to keep her last name as Earp. Keeping Dan's last name meant that she could keep receiving his pensions. As long as they were married in the church, the church would control her life. The second reason was that she did not want the government to control her life outcomes. Changing her name to Maldonado in a civil marriage meant that the government would control her life. Her government checks listing Earp would stop.

The government checks were vital to her monthly, comfortability arrangements. Without these checks, Teresa would need to cut back on some of the perks she enjoyed.

And why should she do that? It wasn't illegal to keep her previous name. She wanted to be known as the widow of Army Specialist Daniel Earp. She was proud to have been married to such a wonderful man who gave his life for his country. If John Maldonado did not object, no one else should either. All John wanted was to be with Teresa for the rest of his life.

Returning to the job market after they were married, John did accept a job with the Federal Aviation Administration (FAA). As an engineer, his job was a project manager of air traffic control towers. He also oversaw those who actually did the construction. All financial backing of the projects must be approved by him.

Even when John must go out of town, he always phoned Teresa a few times per day so they were never out of contact. Although this was what many married people do, John simply could not be apart from Teresa and must hear her voice. His love for Teresa was as immeasurable as any husband could possibly love their wife.

There was one small problem with accepting the job with the FAA and by now the reader should have guessed. They needed to relocate to Washington, DC. Another move!

Another packing up!

CHAPTER 27

As of this writing, now twenty-one years after they were married, John and Teresa live in Northern Virginia, and obviously without Autumn, Timmy, and Joey. They were grown and had their own lives with their own children.

For twenty-one wonderful years together, they've enjoyed a few ups and downs as with any typical marriage. However, there were certain exceptions that not many, and probably only a miniscule few, would experience.

Teresa's problems with multiple sclerosis had been an on-and-off diagnosis for many years. The disease had always remained active where she would lose the feelings in her legs and would require the use of a wheelchair. There were many issues concerning balance, and at first the wheelchair was pivotal to function. At times, she could walk. Although slowly, her movements were always measured. Unfortunately, there were other times where the issue of walking and balance were so dire that she eventually needed the amputation of her second toe on her right foot due to the circulation issues and gangrene.

While she no longer needed the wheelchair, Teresa still required the use of a walker. There were still balance issues. There was still the issue where the brain didn't send the correct signals 100% of the time. The good news was that the MS is finally gone.

Believe it or not, Teresa actually died a third time. She considered this the most important death among the three and for reasons. One would believe that each of her deaths would be important since this obviously would mean that her life would no longer be here on earth.

There were slight moments where Teresa did not want to come back after each death. Being with Jesus Christ in heaven was the ultimate reward. This was always "NOT" the time according to Him. It would be in His time and not hers. There has been chronic pain from all the surgeries, which included spasms in her neck, toes, and voice box. The surgery in her neck was called cervical spine surgery. Due to the many procedures and after time, Teresa had no working discs in her neck. John took Teresa to Inova Fairfax Hospital in Northern Virginia. During her surgery, a device called a Medtronic pump was inserted into the intrathecal space in the spinal column. Once in place, the pump administered baclofen, bupivacaine, and Dilaudid. This was supposed to reduce or eliminate the suffering Teresa experienced during the spasms. Unfortunately, this was not to be.

And as anyone would guess by now, Teresa flatlined…again.

According to Teresa, when she died, she again saw Jesus and had the following conversation:

"We're going again? Can I stay this time?"

The third time, Teresa was able to see more of her family in different places throughout the country. These were relatives she needed to connect with. They needed to understand that if they did not accept fully the Lord Jesus Christ, then all the "crud" in one's life could never be eliminated. There needs to be more interaction with Jesus Christ and Mother Mary if a person would want all the uncleanliness to be removed.

Teresa then saw the soul of her sister Mary who had become a nun before her death. She saw that all the negativity within Mary was gone even before she had become a nun. Mary was truly inspirational and at peace with God Almighty and Jesus Christ. This made Teresa feel so calm and enlightened. When it was time to move on from her family, Jesus took Teresa's hand.

"I will show you the suffering," He said. "You will also see the good and bad in people and you are to relay these messages." Teresa wanted to respond by asking Jesus if this truly meant that she could not stay. Wouldn't it be great if she could do the work while being next to Jesus instead of going back? Wouldn't that be a greater miracle for those who need to hear the word of God Almighty and Jesus Christ?

This would, obviously, not be the time to joke and ask a third time even though she truly wanted to stay with Him. She instead, smiled and listened. Concerning the operation and medication she would receive with the Medtronic pump, Jesus Christ informed her it was not going to help. Teresa must suffer.

In addition to the operation in her neck and cervical spine, Teresa also had additional problems with her lungs. The oxygen in her body could not expel CO_2. This was called carbon dioxide narcosis or inappropriate oxygen delivery. Teresa was constantly short of breath. She was groping for air that could not adjust fast enough when inhaling oxygen and needing to expel the carbon dioxide in a matter of microseconds as normal people.

This is the reason Teresa today required pure oxygen through the nose. With the miracle of medicine of the twenty-first century, Teresa did not have to carry, or drag, a huge oxygen tank. The device was much smaller as she put it in her walker with the tubes inserted into her nostrils.

John was not informed that Teresa had died during the operation. It was not necessary. Teresa came back to life and was resting in post-op. She was in the hospital for a week and a half and went home knowing that she must suffer and be on oxygen.

According to Teresa, this was what God Almighty and Jesus Christ wanted of her during the remaining time on earth. She would inform John of her death at a later date. First and foremost was recuperating from the surgery so she could get out of the hospital.

CHAPTER 28

Teresa's life today was busy but not so busy that she would put her life in jeopardy. There were still medical issues, but none were life-threatening as they were in the past. Her schedule was consistent and rarely without change.

If an appointment were made, it was always kept according to the needs and within the time frame that her prayers were said. Jesus Christ always came first as He would make sure she was happy, informed, and doing what she was instructed to do. She considered this a great blessing. Doing God's work was always preferential over anything that transpired throughout the day.

She went to church every day and preferred the Latin Mass. Since Pope Francis allowed the bishop to determine when and where the Latin Mass would be held, Priestly Fraternity of Saint Peter (FSSP) was the only Latin Mass accepted by the Vatican. For individual and personal reasons, as one would understand, I decided not to mention which Latin Mass Teresa attended or where.

In Teresa's words, "Jesus chimes in with her for twenty minutes every day." She also visits heaven daily. She did not ask when she would finally be with Jesus but had been told that she would have advanced information about the time and day. How wonderful it was, indeed, to be able to know when you would leave the earth plane and be with Jesus in heaven. Think of all the preparation a person could do knowing this information. The only problem others might see would be preparing your family and friends for this ultimate day.

Would Teresa inform them that her time was soon to expire? They might feel totally different than Teresa. They might protest and ask her to speak with Jesus to delay her time. It was a difficult conundrum indeed. However, a grand decision such as this was purely heavenly!

Teresa said that in the present day, she was never depressed. She didn't need it. Jesus did not want anyone to be depressed. All negativity should be removed. Life should be lived in mutual harmony with everyone and anyone. Teresa continued to explain, "All priests remove your sins because they want you to accept Jesus Christ. You are there to fall on your knees and confess and love Jesus. This is the way to eternal life."

One of Teresa's requirements was to pray—pray for intentions and pray for everyone she met. She would ask everyone about their intentions and record them in a writing journal she carried with her everywhere. She prayed always and often.

Everyone who spoke with Teresa would hear the words from Jesus. They knew, instinctively, that they were the blessings of the Lord and the Lord was with her. No one ever disputed or questioned her words. Her face was without stress and crystal clear. Her smile was infectious. Her words were distinct and pure.

And why wouldn't they be? How would you feel if a person came up to you and blessed you and spoke the words of Jesus Christ? Although she was talking with them while dragging around her walker and oxygen, people knew this was not a woman who confronted them in a negative manner.

Her voice was lovely and calming. She could be your doting mother or grandmother depending on how one saw her. Her flowing long light-brown hair hang on her sides and back. Her eyes glistened with a terrific sense that she was quite knowledgeable with the words she spoke. John, though not devout, just let Teresa speak. He knew his wife was so very special. She was a shining emblem of that which Jesus Christ had chosen to be a vessel for Him. Not only did John know she was doing the work of Jesus Christ, but also he knew he was blessed to be a part of her life.

He was also a proud husband—proud in that his wife was showing so many that with prayers, blessings, and beliefs, they could enter into the kingdom of heaven. They could know the ultimate peace and love of God Almighty, Jesus Christ, and the Holy Ghost.

Even if they were not believers, no one ever questioned her words or dismissed her in an act of rudeness or disrespect.

Teresa might ask for your name so she could write in her journal the intentions you asked. She wanted to know your name. She wanted to be able to pray for you. She was totally sincere. She was honest. People simply thanked her and she moved on.

When Teresa and I recently spoke, I needed many of the open spaces within the story closed. I was writing quickly and found disconnected continuity. During the conversation, Teresa joked and quoted, "You can't take the Jew out of the person."

This was a dual reference as she knew, first, that Jesus Christ was obviously Jewish. Christianity did not begin until well after Jesus Christ died. In researching the origins of Christianity, "the earliest followers of Jesus were apocalyptic Jewish Christians. Christianity remained a Jewish sect, for centuries in some locations, diverging gradually from Judaism over doctrinal, social and historical differences. The biblical canon did not become official until 382. The Roman Emperor Constantine 1 became the first Christian Emperor in 313." This was referenced in Wikipedia and stated in the History of Christianity: "Roman Emperor Constantine 1 issued the Edict of Milan expressing tolerance for all religions, making Christian worship legal. He did not make Christianity the state religion but did provide crucial support."

Secondly, Teresa knew that I converted from Judaism. When I went through my conversion in 2015, it was as if I had graduated and was now completed. It was a miraculous feeling for me and my family since my wife is a "cradle" Catholic. I remember the glow on my mother-in-law's face as she was so proud. Teresa informed me that growing up, her parents celebrated Rosh Hashanah (Jewish New Year), Yom Kippur (Day of Atonement), Passover (celebration of the escape from slavery from the Egyptians), Chanukah (Festival of Lights), and all the Jewish holidays. How could you not when Jesus was celebrating them as well? Those who surrounded Jesus, the twelve apostles, Mary, and others, all celebrated every Jewish holiday and the Sabbath.

Today, I have the privilege of contacting Teresa anytime I want. We do not live far from each other and sometimes attend the same Mass. She has been a guiding light, and I look forward to her conversations and texts. One last item that Teresa mentioned to me. She suddenly became hesitant the week before I wanted to send this to my publisher, to have anything negative about Tim mentioned. She has no regrets about her life with Tim. She has forgiven everything he had ever done to her. She has removed all the animosity and ill will.

I informed Teresa that this was not necessary to remove her past from the book. People would want to know since those who picked up the book would want to understand how her journey led her to such a devout, wonderful existence. This is the journey all should strive to reach the quality of life that Teresa has.

Letting Jesus Christ into your life is to show all the qualities and aspirations of reaching heaven. Praying daily and often is a mantra everyone should strive. "The Lord be with you" should not be just words uttered. They should be the means to fulfilling spiritual goals.

AFTERWORD

I asked Teresa for an update on Autumn, Timmy, and Joey. It is important to reference where they are today as they have endured so much over the course of their lifetimes. It is good to know that they absolutely love and adore their mother. Also, the reader would want to know. They have read and been a witness to their life experiences.

Autumn is married to Paul Ward with two adult children. Michelle is twenty-four and Caitlin will be sixteen in April 2024. Timmy has been with his husband since 2012. They were civilly married in 2018. Joey is married to Sean Warner, no relation to Kevin Warner, and has three daughters. Jacqueline turns eighteen in June 2024. Bella Angel turns sixteen in October 2024. Sean's twin sister, Stephanie, passed away. Her daughter, Rylee Joy, was adopted by Joey and Sean. Rylee Joy turns nine in May 2024.

Teresa-Rose Earp is a dear, wonderful friend. When we first met at the Gainesville Diner in Gainesville, Virginia, she informed me that she had been looking for the correct individual to write her story for thirty years. She said she knew I was the right person before she even met me.

Gregory Bain of Northern Virginia and I go to the same Catholic Church. He then said that Teresa also attended the same church. He provided Teresa's phone number and email and said to immediately get in touch with her. I even asked him if Teresa really wanted me to write this. How was this possible?

"When you meet Teresa, you will understand perfectly why she wants you to write her biography. She is amazing!"

Teresa had not read my two previous books of fiction or my two books of spiritual poetry. She hadn't even done research about me.

When I asked how she knew, Teresa simply said, "Jesus told me you were the one."

I am not a well-known writer. This is my avocation as I am a retired telecommunications worker. So I asked her again, "Are you sure you want me to do this? I've never written a biography."

Teresa simply smiled and stated, "Jesus said you were the one. And I always follow Him."

Since then, Teresa has read my other books and has said she enjoyed them and my writing style. I know she is not telling me this for the sake of my ego. She knows I do not need or want that. She knows deep within her mind and body that I will be guided and would not write anything she does not want written.

As I was trying to determine what to write as post remarks for this biography, I was led to 1 Corinthians 1:1–9 (NIV):

> 1 Paul, called to be an apostle of Christ Jesus by the will of God, and our brother Sosthenes, 2 To the church of God in Corinth, to those sanctified in Christ Jesus and called to be his holy people, together with all those everywhere who call on the name of our Lord Jesus Christ-their Lord and ours: 3 Grace and peace to you from God our Father and the Lord Jesus Christ. 4 I always thank my God for you because of his grace given you in Christ Jesus. 5 For in him you have been enriched in every way-with all kinds of speech and with all knowledge-6 God thus confirming our testimony among you. 7 Therefore you do not lack any spiritual gift as you eagerly wait for our Lord Jesus Christ to be revealed. 8 He will also keep you firm to the end, so that you will be blameless on the day of our Lord Jesus Christ. 9 God is faithful, who has called you into fellowship with his Son, Jesus Christ our Lord.

Thank you, God Almighty and the Lord Jesus Christ, for giving me the opportunity to write about Teresa-Rose Earp, your specially chosen disciple. This has been a most enjoyable and humble experience. You have brought me closer to you and to whom I consider a cherished friend.

ABOUT THE AUTHOR

Richard Parnes lives in Northern Virginia with his wife Mila. Writing is not only his avocation but also a spiritual journey of listening and learning to hear the words from God and Jesus Christ. He wants everyone to understand and comprehend his desire to allow others to let down their guard and open up to the wonders of their own spiritual paths.

My Lazarus Life has further enriched his life.